T0171165

MAGIC CITY

MAGIC CITY

TRIALS OF A NATIVE SON

GALLERY BOOKS   MTV BOOKS

NEW YORK   LONDON   TORONTO   SYDNEY

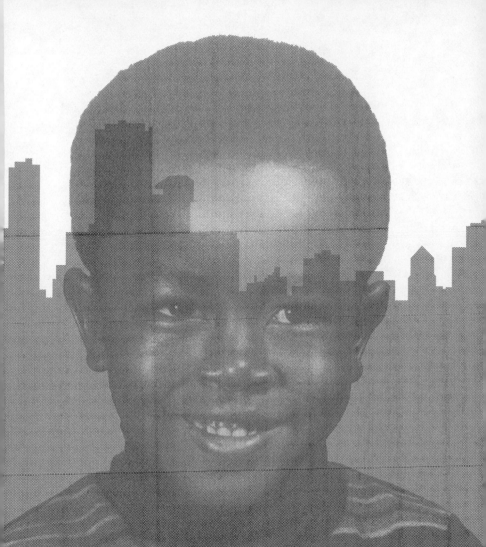

Trick Daddy

WITH PETER BAILEY

Gallery Books
A Division of Simon & Schuster, Inc.
1230 Avenue of the Americas
New York, NY 10020

Copyright © 2010 by Maurice Young and Peter Bailey

MTV Music Television and all related titles, logos, and characters are
trademarks of MTV Networks, a division of Viacom International Inc.

All rights reserved, including the right to reproduce this book or portions
thereof in any form whatsoever. For information address Gallery Books
Subsidiary Rights Department, 1230 Avenue of the Americas, New York,
NY 10020.

First MTV Books/Gallery Books paperback edition November 2010

GALLERY BOOKS and colophon are trademarks of
Simon & Schuster, Inc.

For information about special discounts for bulk purchases,
please contact Simon & Schuster Special Sales at 1-866-506-1949
or business@simonandschuster.com.

The Simon & Schuster Speakers Bureau can bring authors
to your live event. For more information or to book an event
contact the Simon & Schuster Speakers Bureau at 1-866-248-3049
or visit our website at www.simonspeakers.com.

Designed by Akasha Archer

Manufactured in the United States of America

10   9   8   7   6   5   4   3   2   1

Library of Congress Cataloging-in-Publication Data is available.

ISBN 978-1-4391-4852-5
ISBN 978-1-4391-5767-1 (ebook)

. . . Thank God for Jesus . . .

MAGIC CITY

1

Born a Thug

MY LIFE BEGAN WITH PORK-N-BEANS.

I'm not talking about the canned food that most residents
in Anyhood, USA, have in their cupboards. Not the soppy stuff
sitting next to the Kool-Aid and ramen, staples of a diet built on
hard knocks.

History cats say the name came about because the only
meal residents in Liberty Square Houses could afford was pork-
n-beans. The idea isn't that far-fetched. My family's cupboard
was stocked with the cuisine. But the origins stemmed from the
stench that came from a local store that cooked the sloppy mess.
It stunk up the entire projects. Then younger folks coined the
name on whatever color your front door was. Apartments with
blue doors were called Blueberries. Those with green doors

were Green Machine. Mines had maroon doors, called Pork-n-Beans.

It's a stone's throw away from downtown Miami, but the Beans might as well be in a foreign country judging by the way cabbies warn visitors to stay away. I'll admit the place ain't South Beach. The neighborhood lies to the east of the I-95 expressway off exit 6A, Martin Luther King Jr. Boulevard. Drivers usually whiz past the wheelchair-bound beggars before they roll up to their car windows along the exit's service road. You'd think it's hard to ignore a dude with two half-legs and a sign that says A PENNY FOR MY PAIN, THANK YOU. Abandoned corner stores, vacant lots, and crippled-looking palm trees line Sixty-second Street until Twelfth Parkway, where the projects begin.

I lived at 1238 Northwest Sixty-eighth Street with my mother, Pearl Brockington, my ten brothers and sisters, and whichever boyfriend she had at the time, usually some sorry good-for-nothing milking the free AC.

Yeah, I said ten brothers and sisters. That's not counting my other twenty or so half siblings on my daddy's side. He has an unknown number of children, but I'll get to that later.

I was born unceremoniously at Jackson Memorial Hospital on September 27, 1974. There weren't any cameras or festivities when little Maurice Young popped into the world. As a kid I imagined my father holding my mother's hand, cheering her through the delivery, kissing her forehead, and whispering things like "Wow, baby, we did it!" — my parents smiling for the camera as a shot is snapped of a bloody, crying infant.

Then I snap to. I see a doctor hovering over my mother sighing, nurses in the corner shaking their heads. *Just another ghetto child born on the welfare dime waiting to wreak havoc in the projects.* Even if those doctors and nurses didn't say it, I'm sure the thought crossed their minds watching Pearl all strung out, sweat and blood on the delivery table. She was truly a member of the UN even if Ban Ki-moon didn't know it.

Uneducated.

Unmarried.

Unemployed.

Society would have to make room for yet *another* one. Pearl and I were alone. It was just me and my older sister, Tameko. Angela, Zakea, Keyon, Omar, Jhabor, Jermaine, D'Angelo, Tavarus, and Hakeem came later.

With only a seventh-grade education, Pearl turned to what seemed to be her most viable economic option—making babies. From the late 1970s to the early '80s all a teenage girl had to do was have kids and the government took care of her. In a sad and twisted way, babies were like vouchers that got you housing and other goodies. The welfare system was systematically trapping folks into a cycle of poverty with disregard to rehabbing young mothers like Pearl. She had already suffered a life of abuse and neglect. Having kids with men who didn't love her just compounded that pain.

Like many folks in the Pork-n-Beans, Pearl's roots went back to Georgia and the Carolinas. Her immediate family came from a small town in South Carolina, a poor place, the kind that puts a face to the conditions that coined the term "dirty" South. Pearl, alongside her siblings, aunts, and uncles, lived on several acres of land scattered over a five-mile radius. Her father was a typical Southerner of the newly freed generation of blacks. To this day my granddaddy speaks with an obvious uncertainty of his stock in life. He's a typical old man from the South. I've only met him three times, but he left a lasting impression. It's like the shackles broken by my great-granddaddy never left my granddaddy's wrists. Nevertheless, he tried his hardest to turn sour lemons into sweet lemonade. But he couldn't stop the abuse my mother would suffer in that small town.

My relatives lived close together so that they could depend on one another for the day-to-day. A couple of my great-uncles reaped the spoils of living in such close quarters. Those spoils were tender young girls to molest. Pearl never spoke much about the abuse, but it left her scarred.

When the family arrived in Miami, the plan was to gain a foothold in new soil, but they soon found themselves stuck in the same rut minus the windchill. My granddaddy decided to hell with the South and moved to Rochester, New York, leaving my fifteen-year-old Pearl behind to be raised by one of her aunts. The racism dealt to them and other blacks was no different from what they faced in Alabama, Mississippi, Georgia, and the Carolinas. Except for a few liquor stores and bodegas, Liberty City had no businesses. Folks had to head to the suburbs to shop.

A couple of high-profile incidents of police brutality only made things worse. People wanted to change the state of the neighborhood, with its broken sewer pipes and deep potholes. So they cleared way for a *new* city the best way blacks in Miami knew how.

We burned the motherfucker down.

2

Back in the Days

I WAS ONLY FIVE WHEN IT HAPPENED, BUT I STILL RE-
member May 17, 1980, like it was yesterday. Hell, I'm sure
every black person in Miami remembers that Saturday evening.
I've been blessed with a photographic memory. Sometimes I
wish I could forget shit because my memories aren't necessarily
the stuff of daydreams.

It was hot as hell that day. I was in the courtyard playing
with my friends while Scoop was telling a familiar story of the
good old days, when Overtown was a black man's "piece of paradise" in Miami.

"Yeah, that was our little piece! You're damn right it was!"
declared Scoop. "Boy, Billie Holiday would come to the Sir
John and get that thing jumping!" He had this way of nodding

his head real matter-of-fact-like after each declaration. Then he slapped his hand on his knee. Just in case you were misinformed or lacked the knowledge, Scoop gave you Miami Black History 101, his version of course.

"That's the problem with you young-uns," continued Scoop. "Don't know your goddamn history. Walking round here lost."

"I swear your mouth just don't tire, does it?" my mother chimed in. "Those babies don't wanna hear your foolishness."

We sure didn't, but Scoop didn't offer intermissions. He paused for a minute, then delved back into his tall tales. His favorites were always those about the Vietnam War.

When he was sober enough to keep his stories straight, he actually drew a crowd. Like most men from his generation, Scoop was a slave to many vices. Johnnie Walker Black was his poison, his lover, confidant, trusted friend. No woman could have filled the void Lady Liquor occupied in Scoop's heart. Everyone knew something happened to Scoop in Vietnam. Like a couple of my uncles, the dude just wasn't right. They say all of those brothers who went over there got fucked-up. He had a constant twitch, as if he was seeing demons and shit in the corners of his eyes. But like I said, when he was sober, his stories drew a crowd. That Saturday he had an audience.

"Boy, I tell you those women were something else!" he yelled. "Not like these wenches over here giving you lip all the time."

Scoop talked about how he and his buddies "tossed up" those Asian women. Honestly, I don't think any Asian dude would be happy with the juicy details Scoop gave most evenings on their women's "love for chocolate." He went on and on about "chocolate fishing" in "yellow seas." "Oriental diving" is what he called it. He could have spared us the details about how they loved his anaconda, but tact wasn't a part of Scoop's personality. (Actually, his stories of the "comfort women," as they were called, showed just how much women are abused worldwide. Advocacy groups said the Vietnamese and American military new about the forced prostitution and encouraged it.)

At least Scoop got his rocks off in that musty old jungle. He even claimed he had a kid over there. No one in the hood could have pictured a Chinky-eyed Scoop. Now, that would have been some freaky shit. But he said he was 100 percent sure he had a kid and was stacking his chips to make the trip to go back and never return to this "sorry shithole."

We knew he was never making that trip, but folks in the hood have a habit of imagining things to look forward to so they can ignore, temporarily at least, the nightmare surrounding them. It was Scoop's way of coping, I guess.

His next target was the government, Lyndon B. Johnson in particular.

"What a jackass!" he fumed. "I swear to God those crackers go around just pissing everywhere."

My mother warned him to watch his mouth around us kids, but it was to no avail. Scoop was going to vent as much as he damn well pleased.

"I'm gonna tell you what the most messed part is," he continued.

A lady Scoop was friendly with jeered, "What is it Scoop? We've just been dying to hear it." The two had a love/hate relationship. They would bite each other's head off one minute and defend each other to the death the next.

Scoop peered down hard at the ground, then slapped his

right hand on his knee. The Betty Boop tattoo on his forearm is still clear in my mind. Most of the other cats that came home from Vietnam had them. He got his inked by a merchant in a village and came down with a case of hepatitis that nearly killed him.

I used to think, "Damn, that's some cold, hard shit." But something told me that the tat was more a scar of pain than a badge of honor. It told on the madness of that war, the nightmare that haunted him. He came back with his limbs, but his soul was still wandering along the Ho Chi Minh Trail.

"Woman, I'll tell y'all if you'd let a grown man speak! That's the problem with y'all sisters these days. Gloria Steinman or whatever her name is got all ya'll believing in that damn women's rights bullshit."

He continued, "They sent us niggers to clean their mess up!"

A couple of the older cats nodded in agreement. When Scoop felt us youngsters alongside my aunt and mother weren't taking him serious, he turned to those old dudes. Scoop and those dudes were always blaming the "man" for getting Negroes to clean up their mess. In the world according to Scoop, all the roads to the world's problems led to the *man*.

Poverty.

Disease.

Crime.

Somehow that white guy living in his pad beyond the bay over there in Coral Gables, Pinecrest, or on Sunset Island was playing a part. In Scoop's opinion white folks were genetically disposed to getting over on their colored neighbors. Hell, given the way blacks ended up over here in the Pork-n-Beans, it's hard for anyone to disagree.

In the early days, blacks weren't allowed to own businesses in downtown Miami. After working all day at the white-owned businesses, black workers headed across the railroad tracks to Colored Town. The neighborhood was a shantytown. With no running water or proper sanitation it reeked of rats and disease. Nevertheless, the residents turned something out of nothing. Kind of like the way slaves used to sing those Negro spirituals to get them prepped and primed to pick cotton for hours in the grueling sun, folks in Colored Town turned a negative into a positive. We've been doing that ever since we got dragged here from across the Atlantic. We somehow turn our pain into joy, our cries into smiles, then get the world dancing.

Look at the blues. B. B. King looks like he's going through hell on that guitar, but go into any swanky spot like South Beach's Prime 112 or Rue 57 in Manhattan and look at the smiles on those rich folk's faces as they wash down filet mignon with cabernet while King plays in the background.

Hell, even Caribbean black folk turned their songs of struggle into a cross-cultural celebration. You ever wondered why the song "One Love" gets played more than "Crazy Baldhead"? They even rock to "I Shot the Sheriff!" Bob actually sings that he put a cap in some cracker's ass for not letting him grow his weed, but they shuck and jive away to it! So it was in Colored Town.

The folks there somehow turned that rat-infested shithole into a piece of paradise. D. A. Dorsey was one of the main movers and shakers. He used his skills as a carpenter to build homes for blacks much like E. W. F. Stirrup did several years before. Stirrup left the Bahamas at fifteen and soon started mixing in real estate and ended up buying out a white dude he worked for. He rented the homes he owned to newly arriving Bahamians so they could get their foot in the door.

Dorsey took it further. He started buying land throughout the country, even some close to Fisher Island. A brother living close to the ocean was unheard of in those days. Blacks weren't allowed to go to the public beaches, so Dorsey brought it to them. He even opened a hotel, bank, and school for blacks on his way to becoming the city's first black millionaire. Colored Town's main strip was booming.

In the 1930s folks called it Little Broadway. Northwest Second Avenue was what people called the center of the "Harlem of the South." All the greats from Billie Holiday to Count Bassie flocked there after finishing their shows down on Miami Beach, where blacks weren't allowed to stay at the hotels. They got to rocking and grooving right there in the shadows of downtown. The soul food cafés and jazz lounges made Northwest First Court from Second to Twentieth streets the place to be. But the real VIPs hung at the Sir John.

The good times wouldn't last long. Officials decided to run the I-95 expressway right through the heart of Overtown for a faster route to South Beach. Thousands of folks were forced out when the place was flattened. Many moved to Liberty Square, but those white folks in Liberty City saw us coming and freaked the hell out. They built a wall at the south end of the projects to keep us out of their section. Other folks moved to Scott-Carver Houses. *Harlem* died. In place of those famous nightclubs, crack houses now stand. Homeless folks sleep on flattened cardboard boxes in the vacant lots.

Those events landed my family here, in the Beans, forced to listen to Scoop's foulmouthed narration of that history each and every evening. But damn, could you blame him? The truth is folks in Miami never got along. It's what happens when you pack a whole bunch of different people on a patch of land and tell them to work it out in the hot sun.

Most recently, Scoop's anger and that of most of black Miami had turned toward people who looked like us, but in a lighter shade.

The thousands of Cubans who came over during the 1960s had formed their own little thriving city within a city. Hell, our mayor, Xavier Suarez, was Cuban. Now, it's true the government helped them gain their foothold, but it is what it is. The mansions in Coral Gables speak for themselves. They acquired power. Mucho power. Even other Caribbean immigrants who came to Miami around the same time, who were treated even worse than the Cubans, started moving past us. But the consensus in the Pork-n-Beans, the Swamps, Chocolate City, the Blues, and other African-American projects in Miami was that those "exotic *niggas* with strange accents" are coming over here taking the goodies King and Malcolm died for *us* to have.

"They can all go back on the tires they washed up on," folks would say. "Got the *nerve* to call me nigger in the county my granddaddy built and his granddaddy built."

Miami was on fire long before we lit the match that Saturday.

3

Bang, Bang, Bang

Scoop didn't take a liking to being interrupted, but when the first gunshot cracked the night air, everything went silent. A random gunshot on a Saturday in Liberty City was not out of the ordinary, but tonight, the sound ricocheted in our psyche.

On the weekend, kids in the Beans were up to all kinds of mischief. Who really cared that someone took to blowing someone's head off on a Saturday in our neck of the woods? Still, it was too early to be hanging on the corner of Sixty-second Street and Twelfth Parkway to pelt the customers with bottles as they drove in for the product. We usually did that when the sun went down. Back then, the only white people we saw were the ones who cruised the parkway on weekends to cop some weed or blow before heading back to the suburbs in southwest Miami-Dade and anywhere else they felt was as far away as possible from Negroes.

When another shot rang out everyone spilled outside.

Scoop continued, "Like I was saying—"

"Scoop, shut the hell up!" someone yelled. "Ain't nobody tryin to hear that from you right now."

Another shot rang out. Then *pop! pop! pop!*

My mother yelled for me to come inside, but what five-year-old is going to listen to such orders when it's pandemonium outside? Then one of my mother's friends came running up the courtyard. Everyone ran toward him. Even old Ms. Lowery, breathing machine and all, rolled her wheelchair out into the yard.

"What's all this hollering going on?" the old lady asked.

The messenger took a deep breath. He was sweating like a pig staring down a barbecue. He knelt to catch his breath, then rested his hand on Ms. Lowery's armrest.

"Y'all ain't gonna believe this," he said, panting. "It's crazy, y'all."

"Boy, if you don't let it out, I swear on my mammy's tombstone!" warned Ms. Lowery.

"Y'all ain't heard it on the radio?"

"If we did, would we be out here staring at your ugly ass waiting for the news of the damn century?" Scoop fired back.

"They let them go. They free, y'all."

Of course they did.

I don't think I had ever felt pain in a person's eyes, never heard it echo from his cheeks and scream from his chest. But when he said those four words, it was like pain had become a person and smacked everyone in the courtyard squarely on the jaw. Scoop smashed his Johnnie Walker bottle against the wall. His hopes that maybe there was some retribution on the way for his bitter past faded. The look on his face told on his years of hoping for that moment . . . of when he could say, "Damn, *we won*" . . . was gone.

Hope is a dangerous thing. It could lead your ass to the middle of the desert thinking there is a water hole somewhere up ahead, but you'll only die of thirst before you get there. Doubt keeps your ass in the car waiting for help to arrive.

People in the hood use doubt as a defense mechanism. You can't knock a man for thinking there is no sunshine when he lives beneath a constant cloud. When the obvious reality of "I told you so" comes around, it doesn't feel so bad if you hold doubt close.

That Saturday afternoon, everyone thought, for once, that folks in Liberty City, Overtown, and Opa-locka would be vindicated. My mother ran inside to turn the radio on, and sure enough Jerry Rushin was on WEDR telling everyone to calm down and keep the peace. Rushin had been the pulse of the inner city for years, our voice on the radio keeping the temperature of Miami's racial tension lukewarm when it was actually boiling over. But how could Rushin explain four cops caught on tape crushing Arthur McDuffie's head "like an egg" getting to walk away scot-free? No, not even Rushin had the right words to calm years of coiled resentment from getting it up the rear routinely.

Arthur McDuffie was a cool brother. He was the type of brother in the hood just living life and taking it easy. His only vice was motorcycles. Well, not a vice actually, but a brother flossing on top a Kawasaki in the early eighties in Miami? It wasn't something cops took kindly to. On December 17, 1979, he popped a wheelie for the last time. Word around the campfire was that McDuffie whizzed past a cop and had the nerve to give him the middle finger. Reports conflict on whether McDuffie stopped or kept on whizzing by and said to hell with it. When he did finally stop, imagine slave drivers catching Nat Turner on his way to France. Nine cops wailed a can of whup ass on that dude. They jumped on him like he owed them money. They smashed his head with a baton until he fell into a coma and eventually died. McDuffie's mother, Eula McDuffie, told the press the obvious: "They beat my son like a dog. They beat him just because he was riding a motorcycle and because he was black."

The cops ran over McDuffie's motorcycle to make it look like he got his injuries from a crash. Talk about gangster.

My relatives were out there protesting with signs blaring JUSTICE FOR MCDUFFIE. It's sad that it took McDuffie's head getting cracked open to get people off the stoop and out in the street demanding better conditions, but, hell, it was a means to an end. Dr. King and Malcolm would have been proud to see all those folks out there protesting for equality. This was what those cats died for. Miami was the last stop on that civil rights train, and we were hungry for change. The cops were charged and officials moved their trial to Tampa. Up there, they felt those bastards would be safe.

Folks took a break from the usual springtime chitlins cookouts.

It was our time.

There were people who never tuned in to the news a day in

their lives, but now everybody was following the daily coverage of the case of the century. In between a bit of Marvin Gaye and James Brown, Rushin gave updates on the ins and outs of the case.

The trial started on March 31 and it was commotion from jump street. The defense removed blacks from the jury pool. Details about the beatdown shocked the world. Those were some cold-blooded dudes. After pulling McDuffie off the bike, they beat the brother with nightsticks and flashlights.

The one Cuban cop was the most vicious. He sat on top of McDuffie and slammed a nightstick into the back of his head. America was shocked by the news coming from *paradise*. The thing is, those pictures on Miami postcards of pearly white sand beaches and art deco hotels were as foreign to us as the idea that people actually had the kind of money to stay in hotels like that. Then the verdict was read.

Not guilty.

Normally, those two words are beloved in the hood. When your reality always seems one mistake away from the chain gang, those two words serve as a lifeline. That Saturday the words yanked a grenade pin. Those jurors were as good as dead. They drove a spear into the heart of black Miami that's never been removed.

When Eula McDuffie cried in that Tampa courtroom, her tears fell on all of us. News travels fast in the hood. Folks didn't have to wait for the Associated Press to say that once again we got bamboozled. Deejay Iceman tried to calm down the angry callers on the radio, but like I said earlier, no one could stop this hurricane. When a sleeping grizzly bear rises, he will bite your fucking head off.

That Saturday, the crowd kept growing larger in the court-yard.

"It doesn't make any sense to listen to the radio. It'll just get everyone riled up!" my mother said, breaking the silence in the wake of the initial news. Nevertheless, everyone huddled around Scoop's radio. Rushin's voice came over the airwaves asking community leaders to hold a town hall meeting on Monday.

Yeah, hope is a blind leader. It took us into the middle of the Sahara without food, water, or shelter and said find your way back to sanity. If only folks had held on to doubt and looked at history, we would have known those cops would get off scot-free. Instead, everyone sang "Lift Every Voice and Sing" and marched the avenues talking about a change is coming. No one played Sam Cooke that Saturday. In this part of town, the Malcolm X murals along Seventh Avenue seemed to yell. But I'm not sure if even that fiery brother would have condoned what happened over the next four days.

"Hell, what did y'all niggas expect?" yelled Scoop. "This is the South, goddammit. Stop letting those uppity up-North Negroes keep filling your heads with pie in the sky!"

Scoop was right. For all its tropical fanfare, Miami is the last stop in the Deep South. You can call it Alabama, South Carolina, and Georgia with an orange twist.

The next few minutes lasted an eternity. A calm before a mad storm gripped Liberty City. The quietest part of a hurricane is several minutes before the deadly inner wall rips through. My mother kept yelling for me to come back inside, but I did what all the other frustrated five-year-old kids did that Saturday. I grabbed a rock.

I raced to join the crowd that was spilling out toward the avenue. When I reached the parkway, police had blocked off the intersection where the usual white customers trickled in. Someone set a trash bin on fire. All hell broke loose. People threw bottles, rocks, and any other makeshift weapons they could hurl at the passing cars. The street turned into bedlam. They chanted, "Kill whitey! Kill whitey!" and all kinds of other racial shit. The sins of a couple murderous cops brought out the worst in everyone.

Cops roped off a section of Sixty-eighth Street in the middle of traffic where a couple hundred people crowded around what looked like bodies on the ground. I tried to duck past the police barricade, but an officer stopped me.

"Back up, folks, back up!" he yelled. "I'm not gonna tell you guys twice!"

How could this dude expect any of us to respect the boys in blue right about now? They cracked a man's skull on a Sunday morning and got to ride off into the sunset! One lady screamed, "Lord, y'all done kill those poor, innocent people!" A Haitian businessman ran out of his bodega screaming for help.

Debra Getman got away that evening, but Jeffrey Kulp and his brother Michael got caught in a whirlwind. They were just some white kids from Pennsylvania trying to catch a tan in the Miami sunshine. On their way back to their hotel from the beach, they got lost in our hood. With no radio in the car, they cruised right into a death trap. A shower of concrete, bottles, and rocks shattered their windshield. The car swerved and hit the sidewalk, then smashed into an old man and little black girl. Some dudes pulled those two guys out the car and beat the white off them. Debra made a dash for it past my project building, and a couple folks helped her into a cab. Meanwhile, Jeffrey and Michael were being stomped to death. For a solid half hour those dudes were hit with rocks, concrete slabs, and just about anything else that angry crowd could get their hands on. One dude even took a newspaper dispenser and smashed it into Jeffrey's skull.

They didn't stop there. The gunshots we had heard were the ones fired into Jeffrey and Michael. After that, someone drove a Cadillac truck over their bodies. The driver jumped out and jammed a screwdriver in their chests. The devil came to Liberty City. He and his imps removed all the humanity from our projects as the sun began to set.

I stood there trembling, with the madness running around me. Cars were set on fire and smoke clouded the sky. I hid behind a lamppost, hoping it would stay lit, afraid the darkness would just swallow me whole.

Three more people were beaten and stoned to death a short time later. By now, Rushin's pleas on the radio for folks to calm down had faded. The violence spread from my projects to the Scott Carver projects. An old lady's car was overturned and set on fire. Most folks in Liberty City that weekend were actually trying to keep the peace, but the enraged minority was determined. It wasn't safe for anyone to choose the *other* side. No one listened to the radio. The worst state of mind is when you realize that the hope you wanted to hold on to had you living in the dark all these years. You can't reason with a person when the rules they were taught to live by are used against them. Violence begets violence.

That Saturday, it wasn't just white folks who caught the beatdown. A Cuban butcher and Guyanese store clerk were also stomped to death.

I guess the rioting was the community's way of finally taking back their self-respect, but we lowered ourselves to the evil that caused the riot in the first place. People sped down Northwest Twenty-seventh Avenue so they wouldn't get caught in the shower of rocks and bottles thrown from everywhere. Kids ran through the streets carrying rocks as big as baseballs. They threw them at any poor sucker caught in the cross fire. Radio hosts instructed travelers to bypass Liberty City on their way home.

Leaders held a rally in downtown Miami at the Metro Justice Building. Now, ask yourself, whose million-dollar idea was that? Picture more than a thousand angry Negroes who already feel slighted by the police gathered at the very headquarters that represented the system they felt failed them. Initially, it was a peaceful rally, blacks and whites gathered together waiting for some light in this dark hour. Then some idiot cop decided to accidently drive his patrol car over the foot of a black girl, turning the peaceful powpow into all-out chaos. Folks started pelting the officers with bottles and began overturning cars. They threw gas bombs and fired shots in the air. Those cops hightailed it out of there.

The situation was getting crazy in Miami. White- and Cuban-owned businesses all throughout Liberty City were looted and burned to the ground. In a weird way, I felt empowered. The burning and the mayhem made me feel like I was part of something. Standing there behind that lamppost, staring at the brothers yelling "Who's your bitch now!" and "We're not taking this shit no more!" made me feel powerful. I was a kid, but you couldn't tell me I wasn't King Kong at that moment.

Thousands of people were in the streets. People wheeled shopping carts with televisions, stereos, and other appliances.

One dude sold sneakers at the corner of Twelfth Parkway and Sixty-second. It's funny how people can turn righteous anger into a hustle.

The scene on Seventh Avenue was what folks dreaded most. The avenue is what Lennox Avenue represents in Harlem. Stores were flattened. The only life on that strip was the flickering fires that could be seen all throughout the shopping district, but the biggest fire was at Norton Tire Factory. It's where cops beat and interrogated black folks during the 1960s and '70s. Folks took pleasure in lighting that fire.

Jumbo's was one of the few places spared in the riots. The soul food restaurant had its own affinity to Liberty City. It was the first eaterie to be integrated in Miami. The Jewish cat Bobby Flam that ran the place was a straight talker who felt blacks were being disenfranchised. The day he decided to hire black employees, all thirty of his white employees stormed out. Even to this day when asked about his motives, he replies, "It was the right thing to do." That Saturday night, Bobby's electrician called to warn that "there would be trouble later." Bobby told his staff to take the night off. Instead they showed up to guard the place.

By Sunday some white folks started firing back. That's what people don't understand. Violence doesn't have a face to it. You push little Ms. Mary Poppins in a corner and she'll knock your ass out with her umbrella. It is what it is. Even a preacher got whacked that morning. When the National Guard finally got the situation under control on Wednesday, the damage was already done. Eighteen people were dead and the price tag on damages was $100 million. But everyone in Liberty City thought it sent a *message*.

"We're tired of living over here in hell while the rest of y'all enjoy paradise." You might as well have posted that sign on the entrance to Liberty Square Houses. In the courtyard Scoop bragged about how "they gotta take notice now." He even seemed sober for an entire week.

My mother didn't speak much about the riots, but I know she felt black folks lowered themselves to the level of those murderous cops. I think everyone in the projects felt that way. Like I said earlier, McDuffie was a cool brother, and it was an unspoken truth, but everyone knew he wouldn't have wanted to know his death caused innocent people to die. It caused more mothers to lose sons and a neighborhood to lose its humanity, but sometimes the means justify the ends. Folks were sure officials would take notice of the neglect that caused Liberty City to be rotting from the inside out while fancy skyscrapers were sprouting all over Miami. The neighborhood wouldn't go unnoticed anymore and businesses would come to Liberty City. The means did cause a lot of pain, but we were used to that shit in our corner of the city. Now, we wanted the life we saw on those commercials and postcards about Miami.

But when the smoked cleared, we were still left with Pork-n-Beans.

4

Ain't No Santa

BROKE WOULD HAVE BEEN A NICE WAY OF DESCRIB-
ing my family's financial situation. I could think of a better
phrase to paint a full picture of Pearl's predicament: no pot to
piss in. When the electricity was on, the thirteen-inch, black-
and-white television didn't work.

When you had a large family in the Beans, housing officials
gave you an extra apartment. So they tore down the wall of the
adjacent apartment to make room for Pearl and her clan. Government cheese, powdered eggs, and the other fine cuisine food
stamps afford made for dull dining. My mother never worked.
I know that raises a red flag with most hardworking American
folks, but I'm proud of my mother nonetheless. She did her
best to provide for eleven kids. Sometimes people are dealt one

sorry deck of cards. Society may look at Pearl as everything that's wrong with the inner city. Folks may paint her as the face of the welfare cartoon skit. Pearl would star in the one in most people's minds of a teenage girl who wears hair curlers and chews a big stick of bubble gum, with a tribe of nappy-headed kids tugging at her skirt.

If that's what people want to see on the surface, I'm okay with that because they don't know Pearl and the sacrifices she made to put food on our table when there were no food stamps. I won't shed light on those things in fear of furthering the comedy skit already etched in people's minds, however much of a good laugh it provides.

We slept on three mattresses all huddled together. My mother slept on the couch. I snuggled up to her some nights when I saw her cry. Pearl is a strong woman. She never really cries like most people do. No tears flow when her heart seems heavy. But I felt her pain. I know that may sound all soft and shit, but it is what it is. I'm my mother's oldest son, and for the most part it's safe to say I raised her. That sounds suspect, but in hoods all across America young brothers are burdened with doing much the same thing. I'm not special.

My mother has ten different baby daddies. It's a past that made her distrustful of men. She didn't keep a man. So you know drama was always a stone's throw away. I'm not sure if Pearl was just genetically disposed to picking losers or she consciously did so to avoid having to get close to anyone.

Let me explain. Some people actually choose people they know will be trouble from jump street so they have an out when things get heavy. Regardless of the reason, my mother's battles with men were legendary.

"No-good suckers," my mother called them. "All your daddies are a bunch of sorry bastards."

Pearl wasn't one to hold her tongue. I guess that's why none of the men hung around long. If you wanted a war, my mother would give you the bullet, gunpowder, and rifle. She liked a good fight. Our apartment wasn't large by any means, so you know when she and one of her boyfriends got into it. The whole Beans would know.

A typical scenario had her throwing one of those lousy dudes out with people peeking out their doors to witness the *WWE Raw* prime-time special *Pearl vs. Sorry Baby Daddy, Part III*. One guy in particular, Ralph, couldn't get enough of the abuse. I mean, even I used to feel sorry for the guy. I still can't tell you what Ralph's occupation was. He had one of those "all of the above" résumés. A lot of folks around my way had that work history. Leaky faucet? I got you. Broken television? I got you. Concert tickets? You get the point.

"What's cracking, young blood?" I hated when he called me that. *I am the man of the house, dammit, even if you fools think I'm not past puberty.* "Your mama, Pearl, around?" I always wanted to tell the bastard, "No, go bum food stamps from another single woman with kids! We're in the projects. I'm sure you'll find plenty of options." But I knew my place, and besides, old Ralph had a sense of humor.

The truth is, I wanted a father figure. When you're alone in the projects with your mom, you envy the kids whose father stuck around. In the ghetto pecking order—*yes, there's such a thing*—kids whose father and mother live together always feel they have one up on the kids who don't have that. Because most likely, they know your father may have been a shot caller who simply took advantage of your mother and kept it moving. He probably lived in a big house with his *real* kids married to the woman he *really* wanted. Yeah, it's sad but it's true. Even in the projects where everyone is at the bottom economically and sociologically, markers say who's at the bottom of the bottom.

Pearl and her clan were the residue in the pan. So much so the social services people always came to check up on us. I hated that. Let's be honest, those social services folk rarely give a damn. It's a shitty job and the pay sucks. Do you really think some caseworker enjoys driving to the Pork-n-Beans once a month to see how poor Kiesha is making out with little Ray Ray and the flock? Hell no! In their opinion Kiesha should have kept her damn legs closed or used birth control, which they gave out in schools those days.

Our caseworker was Ms. Ridley. I had a crush on the lady. (Well, I had a crush on pretty much everything in a skirt and two legs, even in those days.) So when she came knocking on our door, I ran up all polite and shit and said, "Welcome to our humble abode."

"Boy, move out the way!" my mother would yell. "That lady doesn't have time for your foolishness!"

Pearl doesn't fancy a lot of people, but she despised Ms. Ridley. It probably was because Pearl saw an image of what she could have become before she found herself stuck on welfare with us.

"How are you making out, Pearl?" Ms. Ridley would ask.

"I told you we're just fine. I don't know why you people have to always keep coming around here."

"I keep coming because it's my job and I care, Pearl. I know it must be hard being a young woman with all these children to take care of."

"You don't know a damn thing! You don't know your ass from a can of beans!" yelled Pearl. "Coming around here like you really give a damn. Lady, spare me!"

Pearl has a fiery temper. You bring the artillery and she'll start the war. "Pearl, maybe you just need some counseling. There's a great program where you can even take classes while someone watches the kids."

"Lady, what I need is for you to hurry up with your walk-through so you can kindly leave my house!"

Ms. Ridley shrugged.

I felt sorry for the lady. She seemed to have our best interests at heart, but Pearl just thought she was an up-North "patroniz-ing bitch." I believe Ms. Ridley was educated somewhere in New Jersey, and back then Southern folks didn't take kindly to what people round my way called "uppity ways." It's funny how even back then and to this day behaving like you have some good sense and home training is frowned upon in the hood.

My favorite part came after my mother would give Ms. Ridley the third degree. Pearl would go to the kitchen, leaving Ms. Ridley all to myself. I guess you could call it my first ren-dezvous.

"Come here, Maurice. How's the little man of the house doing?"

"I got everything under control," I answered, nodding my head.

"That's my boy. Your mother is under a lot of stress, so it's up to you to take care of her, okay? Can you do that for me?"

"I think I can."

Then Ms. Ridley gave me the biggest hug. I guess the crush I had on her wasn't the boy-likes-girl type. Looking back, I think my affection toward that caseworker and several others that would float through my life came from the fact that someone actually gave a *damn*. It might sound clichéd, but stuck in that crummy apartment with my mother and brothers and sisters, I felt lost. You look outside and everyone around you is pretty much in the same rut. There was no *love* in the Pork-n-Beans. It was just people scraping by. So when someone from the outside visited, it was like I got to take a field trip to some faraway land.

Ms. Ridley didn't live in the projects, or close to them for that matter. She was well-educated but she looked like us. She was black. Back then, we didn't get to meet black folks who actually went to college. I know my mother felt Ms. Ridley was just doing her *job*. Maybe she was. Or maybe I was just a number on a pad she had to check off on her daily visits, but the hug was a gift. In those five fleeting seconds or so, it made me feel important. It made me feel like I wasn't just some nappy-headed bastard child trapped in the hood.

Then she went home.

I don't think my mother actually disliked Ms. Ridley. I believe every time she or any other social worker came around, it caused fear that my brothers and sisters and I were on the verge of being split up. At times when Ms. Ridley came, the water or electricity was off. Sometimes they were off at the same time. Sometimes she came by when Pearl and Ralph or some other boyfriend were arguing. Those factors didn't bode well with the child services people always lurking. Of course, Pearl's predicament could easily have been taken care if my father or one of my siblings' fathers had assumed the man's role, but they were all too busy being a statistic.

Only two of my siblings share the same father. What was the sum total of those ten guys' financial and emotional contribution to our well-being? Zero. I hated those men. I know it's a strong word, but feeling abandoned in that rat-infested apartment took its toll. There is a reason why black boys raised with single mothers are prone to killing other black boys. You don't have to take my word for it. Do your research. Here's my theory. If your first images of black men are of those who leave your mother stuck on skid row without a pot to piss in, then you'll assume a hatred for your likeness. You grow up believing that brothers will tear you down, so you try to destroy them before they destroy you. It ain't rocket science. I know it sounds like some twisted, fatalistic mumbo jumbo, but it's real. Go to any prison in America and take a survey of what the inmates think of their fathers. That's if they even knew the cat. If I could have killed one of those dudes, I would have. Now I'm not saying there aren't exceptions to that rule. But a boy's chances of becoming a success increase when he has a blueprint to follow.

Dating options for an unemployed woman with eleven kids are slim to nonnegotiable. It takes a special kind of man to even consider a woman with that kind of baggage. Only a man who was willing to look past what others see as damaged goods would take on such a challenge. His name was Lucious. He was my mother's long-term boyfriend. He was in the military and what you could call a man's man. Every time Lucious paid a visit from being away on his tour of duty, it was like Superman had entered the Beans. Well, to me at least. In those days, a brother in the military meant he was doing something. Most cats from the hood didn't have the financial means to go to college so they did the next best thing and bore arms. It was an honorable path to becoming all you can be, I guess. When Lucious arrived, my mother rolled out the red carpet. Inside, she laid out a dinner with candied yams, roast beef, peach cobbler. Like I said, it was really as if Superman had entered. I would run into the bathroom when he knocked on the door.

"Hey, baby." He kissed Pearl on her cheek. "Where young blood at? Where my little man at? Where he hiding? I got something for him."

"I told you stop spoiling that boy," my mother answered.

All the while I listened behind the bathroom door. I got happy every time Lucious asked for me. I respected Lucious and knew I was his favorite. Yeah, I was special to Lucious.

"What's happening?" I said sheepishly.

"What's happening!?" he sarcastically replied. "Oh, all of a sudden you ain't excited to see old Lucious?"

Of course I was. But I wanted to show him I was a man, and men don't show emotion. He pulled out a toy German soldier as my mother went into the kitchen.

My eyes lit up.

"Yeah, I knew this would get you to smile," he whispered. "Now go put it under the bed so your mother won't see."

I tucked it under the mattress, alongside the other trinkets Lucious had brought back from the places he had visited. Lucious knew I had never seen anything beyond Twelfth Parkway. The gifts were his way of expanding my view of the world.

After staying for however long his tour of duty gave him, he would give my mother some cash. She was always reluctant to take it. But he insisted. Lucious always tried to be the rock in our storm when he came around. Honestly, he was that eye in the hurricane. Sadly for us, he and my mother could never get it together. That left me with big shoes to fill as Pearl's oldest son. It gave me a title too often held by shorties in the Beans and other projects across America—head of the household.

5

Count My Money

You learn early in the hood that cash flow is the name of the game. You ain't shit without dollars, pesos, gwap, dinero, or whatever else they call money these days. We've all seen the commercials and sappy movies touting money as the root of all evil and how it can't make you happy and all that. But you ever notice that the guy featured in those behind-the-fame Hollywood stories always has the epiphany after crashing numerous Ferraris and boning tons of supermodels? It's never the guy working at the counter in McDonald's singing the whole "money can't make you happy" song.

Exactly.

He wants to experience the hot cars, fine chicks, and whatever else the cash can afford so he can test that theory out on his own. I needed to get mine. So I figured it was time for me to get a hustle. Pierre's Thrift Grocery became a cash cow.

My mother, Scoop, and aunts were always trying to sucker some kid into running to the store to get something for them. The laundry list included Newports, beer, and potato chips. Folks were always harassing us kids to run to the store. I especially hated the runs to get tampons. Pierre's was just one block across the Twelfth Parkway, but if my mother and her friends were watching an episode of *Good Times*, I became their errand boy. So much so the cashier at the store found it humorous.

"Damn, are you the black Speedy Gonzales?"

I heard it all.

But I had an idea to turn my shuffling back and forth into a business. It dawned on me that most folks would forget to ask for their change until I brought it up. So, I decided to charge them $1 per run. It doesn't sound like much, but like I said before, it all adds up. I even added on surcharges for what you might call extreme working conditions. Runs before sunset cost $1. Runs after sunset were $1.50 because that's when most of the shootings in the hood went down. I charged $1.75 for a half hour before the store closed.

People's priorities in the projects can be really warped. Folks wouldn't save their money to get up out the hood, but they had $5 to give a seven-year-old to run across the street to buy cigarettes. I can't tell you how many times Fat Boy Slim sent me to get a Snickers bar, Jujubes, or pork rinds. He would have done better to open a junk-food store in his own apartment, given the amount of calories he soaked up each night. But those calories amounted to cash in my pocket.

A true hustler has to have more than one gig, of course. No

one told me that seven-year-olds couldn't work in the stockroom at Winn-Dixie, so I settled for bagging groceries. After school I raced to aisle 13. For those of you who have never bagged groceries, there's a science to it and a pecking order, if that's what you want to call it. There isn't any money to be made in the express lanes because obviously there aren't a lot of bags to carry out in shopping carts. The store manager was this Haitian guy named Jean. He was a pretty cool dude when he wasn't schooling all of us bag boys on the lack of "home training" American kids suffer from. I think he liked me from the beginning because I worked hard. But good old Jean had a more practical reason for making me his favorite. A large community of well-to-do Haitians lived in the suburbs in southwest Miami-Dade. Jean and the rest of the less fortunate ones were toughing it out up here with us several blocks around the way in "Little Haiti," a reality I don't think Jean was happy about. I was underage so he didn't have to pay me as much as the other bag boys. Early on, I learned that in this world people will try to get over in any way they can. Some people exist within the rules of the system. Others bend and manipulate those rules to make the system suit their needs. The latter become the bosses in society. Do your research if you don't agree. Alongside exploiting me, however, he did occasionally throw in some good advice. "Remember customer service," he told me. "People tend to open their wallets when you make them smile."

After that, I always beamed a big one at the end of the cashier line. I made sure those shoppers saw my pearly whites. You cashed in when an old lady came to the register. On the way out you usually had to endure a lecture on how "you kids today are getting screwed up," but for the most part it was a pleasant exchange. Most shoppers gave me a $.50 tip. The really cheap ones flipped a quarter. Some bastards gave me nothing. Can you believe that? I bagged your groceries, quite neatly I should add, making sure the eggs are at the bottom so they don't break, and you can't scrounge up a nickel? Some folks just had no class. But the old ladies were always the most generous. On occasion I got a dollar.

I wasn't doing too bad if I helped twenty customers. I used to laugh all the way to the shoebox I stashed my cash in. I kept it in the vents in the roof of our apartment. With people going in and out of there like it was the Beans Holiday Inn, I had to make sure my money was secure.

I was pretty proud of my store-errand franchise. I was surprised no other kid had come up with the idea. When I and the other bag boys at Winn-Dixie got into an occasional spat over whose turn it was, Jean usually quelled the situation before it turned to blows. It was easy, trouble-free moneymaking.

At the end of the night, sometimes Jean treated me to a soda or Snickers bar from the vending machine. But my hustle didn't end there. After bagging groceries I rode my bike over to the Fire Star gas station at the corner of Sixty-eighth Street and Tenth Avenue.

The scene at the gas pumps outside Fire Star wasn't drama-free. The cashier inside could care less about the homeless panhandlers that harassed the drivers as they drove in to fill their tanks. He cared even less about some kid from the Beans getting roughed up by one of them.

Sticks and Doc were regulars. I don't remember much about their personal lives, but I know for sure life had dealt them a bad hand. Sticks was a rail-thin, half-dead-looking dude that a lot of customers felt sorry for so they let him pump their gas and clean their windows. Seriously, Sticks always looked like he was just one breath away from the graveyard, always coughing and shit.

Doc was a problem. That dude was scary. He was always talking to himself and shit. Word on the street was that he dropped out of medical school after his fiancée cheated on him. Who knows? I just made sure I didn't cross him. The gas station lost a lot of business because of his antics. Doc didn't take a liking to people telling him they didn't want him pumping their gas. He gave one schoolteacher a treat I'm sure she will never forget. Hell, I'm sure that lady recounts this story to this very day.

She pulled up in her Toyota and got out singing one of those old gospel hymns. You know, the one where you're told to lay your burdens down at the cross. Well, Doc came over and was polite at first.

"Ma'am, let me get that for you," he said. "You wouldn't want to get your clothes smelling like gasoline."

"I'm fine, thank you," she replied.

Doc was accustomed to some reluctance. There could have been any number of reasons why people said no. Like I said, the dude just wasn't right. So folks normally got scared, rolled their windows up, and waited for him to finish so they could speed off.

He leaned in. "Come on, lady, I'm just out here trying to earn a decent living. Let me get that for you." He reached for the pump.

"Oh, I've heard that before!" she snapped back. "This is what you call a decent living? You're nothing but a lazy lowlife trying to score an easy buck!"

"You don't know me, lady!" Doc fired back.

"Yes, I do! People can't go to the store much less the gas station without you bums harassing them!" she yelled.

"I got your bum, bitch!"

What happened next lives on in infamy. That lady picked the wrong homeless guy to insult that day. I'm sure she still wishes she had let good old Doc pump her gas. All she had to do was get in her car and put the radio on to her favorite gospel station, then drive off. Doc backed away. The lady turned away from him and continued singing. Then it happened. It was as if those lady's insults had dug up some deep-rooted resentment Doc had harbored all these years. That schoolteacher should have known it's never good to point the finger at someone's circumstances, especially when you have no clues as to how they arrived there. She didn't get the memo. The next thing we knew that lady was getting a yellow shower. Yes, Doc pissed on her. He hauled out his ding-a-ling and soaked her. I don't even think that lady realized what was happening until a good ten seconds into the drenching. She screamed until the cashier ran out with a baseball bat and chased Doc away from the station.

Standing there, soaked from waist down in Doc's piss, that lady was a sight. She cried and cried. Myself, Sticks, and the cashier did what any other upstanding gas station attendants would have done. We laughed and laughed and laughed some more. I was laughing so hard, my stomach cramped up. She jumped in her car and sped off. It just goes to show you that every dog has his day. We never saw Doc again, but I'm sure for those several seconds he felt like he had taken back some form of his dignity.

With Doc out of the picture, business ran a bit smoother

for me. I learned to stave off the competition from panhandlers by simply breaking them off some of my tips. Most were bad for business anyway because, like Doc, they scared away customers. Already, I was learning how to control the market.

Every hustler knows that to gain you have to lose. Anyone that isn't willing to break bread won't make bread. It's a catch-22 but a necessary one. When I got the homeless cats on my side, the cashier even took notice and gave me certain privileges. He gave me an occasional free bag of potato chips or a soda, which I shared with Sticks and the other cats at the pump.

My favorite customer was Drop Top Mo. He was cold as ice. I had never seen someone so fly in the hood before. When he cruised down the strip, he transformed it into a movie set. Lights. Camera. Action. Few were flashier than Mo. He would speed through in a blue Mercedes with the titties poking out. That's what we call it when you drop the top on a convertible. Mo had plenty. He would chop the top off every car he drove. Back then a red-candy-painted Chevy Corvette cruising through Liberty City drew a crowd. Mo had about four of them in different colors.

When he pulled up in the Bentley with Gucci interior, everyone rushed the car. It sat on twenty-two-inch rims that could blind a blind man. The chick sitting in his passenger seat was just as fly. The rims weren't the only things that glittered. He wore a long gold-rope chain with a diamond-encrusted medallion. The diamond ring on his pinkie finger was just as huge as the rocks in his pendant.

Sticks and the panhandlers would rush the car as if Jesus himself had arrived. Actually, it *was* like Jesus had come to Fire Star. The cashier peered from behind the counter and shook his head. Other customers rolled their windows up and locked their doors while I soaked it in.

I asked Mo if I could touch the car's leather interior. I bobbed my head to the bass rocking the trunk. Inside sat twin Pioneer speakers I had never before seen. I stared at my reflection in the chrome-colored spinning rims.

"She's a stunna, ain't she? Yeah, this my baby right here," said Mo.

"Wow, how much one of these cost?" I asked.

He stared at me, then chuckled. "More than your life, young blood. Nah, just kidding. She cost me a pretty penny."

Mo never noticed that I took extralong to pump his gas. My favorite part came at the end when he pulled out a wad of cash held together by a diamond-enrusted money clip. He counted hundreds, even thousands. I had never seen so much money. Mo would hand me a twenty, sometimes a fifty. He was always a generous dude to me and the other shorties in the hood.

He jumped in the Bentley and revved the engine. "Sounds like she's singing, don't she?" he boasted.

I nodded. I imagined it was me sitting next to that bodacious babe. She had a rack of melons on her that could make any man drool. As they sped off down the avenue, I stood transfixed in a daydream clutching that $50 bill. I liked how it *felt*. I wasn't sure how Mo came into so much money, but I would soon find out. Folks in Miami were always talking about my half brother Hollywood. Word on the street was that he was the youngest dude in Miami with the same cheese as older cats like Mo. For now, Hollywood's wealth was but an urban legend in my mind. Thus far, everyone around me was broke as hell. Of course I wanted to meet him, but I took the stories with a grain of salt.

Then the station manager snapped me out of my daydream. "You lost your damn mind!" he yelled. "Put the pump up! You're wasting my gas!" He pointed to my soaked sneakers. I had got so lost in my dream of squeezing those melons I was still clutching the gas pump. Gasoline was everywhere. Habib looked at me. He shook his head, then motioned to my pants pockets.

"No, I just made this tip!" I insisted.

"It's not my fault you lost focus with the pimp of the city."

I dug deep into my pocket and handed over the fifty.

"It's like they say, Maurice, easy come, easy go," he said. "Everything that glitters isn't gold, my young friend." At the time I didn't *see* what Habib was trying to tell me. It was a subtle warning that he hoped would register in my mind.

I was ten. He was just a dude with a fucked-up accent getting free labor out of me, Sticks, and all the other Liberty City cats hustling for a buck while he soaked up the AC inside. Now he had the nerve to take the biggest tip I ever got. Fuck Habib.

6

I Got Plans

I JUMPED ON MY BIKE AND PEDALED HOME. I USUALLY got home around eleven. Although the station closed at ten o'clock, I hung out in the neighborhood until I knew everyone in my house had gone to bed. The fighting between my mother and whoever she was dating after Lucious left made home a war zone. Lucious brought stability in a world that was already unraveling around me.

If you see a kid hanging on the corner while you're driving through the hood on your way to the suburbs, he's not necessarily up to no good. His home probably isn't a happy place. He's not trying to rob you. He's just out there trying to soak up some peace of mind. I know it sounds crazy that out in those gritty streets, amid those you learn to sidestep in the daylight, a kid might actually be trying to find temporary respite from the bullshit at home.

You'd be surprised. It's where I learned a lot about life. I would sit on that rusty bench in the middle of the courtyard. Most projects have one. It's mostly reserved for the HNIC, the head nigger in charge, that pimp or drug dealer who perches out there with his crew so he can survey his domain.

At night the throne was left vacant for little old me. The things you see after sunset in the projects can be downright scary. I used to think, if there is a God, why did He stick my family here? It's like He didn't like *us*.

I watched television, so I had an idea of what life *could* be like. The truth is most kids in the Beans sat glued to the television because it was like taking a field trip. For that half hour or so when *Leave It to Beaver* came on, you pretended to be Beaver. It drowned out the gunshots as well as your mother and her boyfriend's screaming. But you never actually thought you could get *there*. No, those people on the tube were just characters that lived in some fantasy world you were never going to visit. That's why I liked Lucious. He had actually visited some of those places in la-la land.

At times I resented Pearl for not maintaining a healthy relationship with him. Nevertheless, I chalked it up for what it was. When I left the courtyard and got home, Pearl was sometimes still awake. I saw the uncertainty in her eyes while she looked over my brothers and sisters as they slept. She sat wondering how she would take care of us all. It made me enjoy giving her some of the cash I earned in my burgeoning enterprises. She was never good with expressing her emotions unless she was hollering, but I knew she was proud of me. "You're becoming a responsible man around here," she would say. "At least you're not turning out like those other sorry niggas."

As many issues as I've had with my father and those of my siblings, I always felt my mother did us a disservice when she talked bad about them. Looking back, I soaked it in like any other kid would do. But the habit of making kids pawns, traded back and forth when the chess game of love goes bad between adults, is a tragedy. Kids should be excluded from the bitter feuding. Unfortunately, the drama plays out on daytime television throughout the week. Ratings go up when those talk shows show a teenage girl calling some dude sorry for not stepping up to take responsibility for the child he may or may not have fathered.

If the first thing that a kid witnesses is his mama and daddy fighting, do you think he'll learn to have healthy relationships with the opposite sex? I'm sure you can answer that question. But since I was indeed the man of the house as a ten-year-old, I enjoyed filling in where those guys didn't. When my mother gave them a tongue-lashing, it showed me just how much more needed I was.

King Kong didn't have shit on me.

Pearl even gave me the idea for my next venture—raking grass. In the hood folks take their lawn seriously. It isn't like there were any manicured lawns in the Beans, but there was a patch of grass outside the front door in front the garbage bin. Remember when I talked about different markers of hood status earlier?

That patch of grass was one such marker. In Anyhood, USA,

you don't violate a man's patch of grass. In much the same way you "never touch a black man's radio," you sure as hell don't mess up his lawn. Seriously, people have got shot over letting their pooch crap on someone's lawn. People could be living in a crummy project apartment, but their lawn would be litter-free and bright green. Some folks even got fined in the Beans for overusing the water to nourish their lawns.

"That's where the money's at, son," Pearl would tell me. "And always make sure you tend very well to the old folk." My mother always talked about taking care of women and the elderly. She drilled that into my skull.

I grabbed my rake and knocked on doors. I even employed a couple of the other shorties in the neighborhood. It was a simple pitch: "Your grass could be the greenest and cleanest in the hood" for an unbeatable price from $.50 to $2 depending on how long it took me to complete the job. The elderly got a discount. Mrs. Lowery was one of my most loyal clients. She sat in her wheelchair and watched me scurry back and forth. I made sure every candy wrapper, soda can, and newspaper was thrown away. She beamed a broad smile at how fast I worked.

"Ma'am, is there anything else I can do for you?" I asked her when I was done.

"No, it looks just fine. I'm so happy for the help." She usually brought me a tall glass of water when I was finished. Honestly, I think old Mrs. Lowery just liked the company. Sometimes her grass didn't need raking at all. Her husband had died, and folks said her son had gotten a football scholarship, went off to college, and never came back. I don't blame him. He probably saw the cookie-cutter homes and manicured lawns on that lily-white campus and screamed hallelujah! The suburban air must have smelled pretty damn good.

With my pockets getting fatter I gained a strut to my step. I was feeling like a million bucks even if my pants pockets were only jingling with coins when I walked. But as the summer loomed, my real hustle was right around the corner.

7

Ghetto Superstar

EVERY HOOD HAS AT LEAST ONE CAT LIKE BOONER or Junior. These are the cats who see little brothers on the corner drifting. In the absence of organized programs they scrounge something together to give the kids something better to do besides "shooting and robbing." They see the potential in lost causes. They may have been that lifeline for a 50 Cent, Lebron James, Russell Simmons, or some other successful brother who could easily have gone the wrong way. It could be the dude that turns an abandoned warehouse into a boxing ring where the shorties can punch out their frustrations, the teacher who runs a basketball league on the weekends. Booner and Junior offered newspapers.

Those cats are never given a community service award at

the swanky black-tie ceremonies. Those spectacles are usually reserved for the crooked politician who opens some rec center in the hood and slaps his name on it and never returns until election time. No, you'll never read about Old Man Booner and Junior in the *Miami Herald*. When they picked me up at Fire Star, I was being a hard-ass like most boys who thought they could tough it out on their own.

I told Sticks to watch the pumps so I could use the bathroom. I didn't need to use the bathroom at all. I went back there to count my tips. Counting money in public was like a death wish. You never know who's watching. People in the Beans were struggling. Folks were getting shot over less than $10.

When I got back, Sticks was arguing with some old dude driving a white van. He made a gesture for the van to keep driving.

"What's up, Sticks? Everything cool?" I asked.

"No, these two old geezers tying up the pump. They won't drive off."

I turned to Booner. Standing there, hands folded, he looked old enough to be my grandfather.

"Y'all heard the man. If you don't need gas, please keep it moving," I warned.

"Oh, you're the boss out here?" Booner asked.

"Yeah, I guess you could call me that. But that really ain't none of your damn business." Up until that point I can't say I backed down from anyone or anything. I didn't take kindly to being pushed around by anyone. These dudes were going to *respect* me.

"Boy, you know what time it is? Your mama know you out here?" asked Booner.

"I'll say it louder 'cause it seems you're hard of hearing. My business is my damn business."

"Young blood does have a point there, Boon," said Junior.

Booner jumped back in the van and started the engine. "Yeah, his business is his business. I was just wondering if he wanted to make a couple extra dollars. Oh, well."

Before the van could lurch forward, I blurted out, "How much are you talking about?"

"That depends on how hard you're willing to work," answered Junior.

I looked back at Sticks. He nodded. In a weird way I knew Sticks thought it wasn't safe for me to be out there at Fire Star. He didn't want me to fall into the traps that led him to be taking orders from a fresh ten-year-old. Yeah, me and Sticks were friends. I guess he liked the fact that I never judged him. I broke bread with him. When he nodded, it was his way of telling me, "Get the fuck outta here." I jumped in the van and never saw Sticks again. My shift at Fire Star was over, for good.

"Boy, what you doing out here this late anyhow?" Booner dug into me.

"My mama told me never talk to strangers. You guys look like strangers."

Booner chuckled. Folks in the hood knew I was fresh. I had a slick mouth. You could say I was witty.

"Ain't your mama Pearl?" asked Junior.

"Yeah, he look just like Pearl, don't he?" replied Booner.

"You got something to say about my mama!?" I snapped back.

"Nah, young blood, just seeing where you get it from."

When they dropped me off, Booner gave me firm instructions.

"We're picking you up at six a.m. sharp. If you're not ready, you don't make the cash." He didn't have to worry. I stayed up all night wondering what those two old cats had in mind, guessing on what the big moneymaking heist could be. Still a minor, I was sure they wanted me to boost some stereos out of someone's car or drop off some kind of *package* to a customer. Older hustlers in the neighborhood were always looking for young shorties with heart to run *errands*. I fit the bill.

Whatever it was, I knew I would score big. I thought about the things I could buy with the pesos. It was time to retire our black-and-white television. The thing got pounded so much it had a dent the size of the Grand Canyon. An old wire hanger served as the antenna. Or maybe I could get the new Atari. A new TV and game system would make me the talk of the Beans. The grand idea Booner and Junior had to make me *rich* was newspapers.

"Y'all got to be kidding!" I yelled when Booner and Junior picked me up that morning. "Y'all think I'm about to go walking around in the hot sun selling newspapers!? Let me out!" I was on my way to becoming wealthy one newspaper at a time. My chariot to riches was equally disturbing. The van was moldy inside with no seats. It was hot as a skillet of fried chitlins and smelled just as bad. In the middle of the summer with no air-conditioning, that van most certainly was going to be where I died of a heatstroke.

That's when I met O'Sean and Darryl. We would soon become connected at the hip. I used to bump into them on the basketball court in the Beans, but we never spoke. I had got into a fight with Darryl over a customer at Winn-Dixie before Jean saved him from a can of whup ass. Honestly, Darryl would have kicked my ass, but I would have given him a run for his money. Young cats like us were always scrapping to prove something to the older dudes. The hardest among us would get the attention of OGs.

Now we were stuck on the same team sitting side by side on the floor of Booner's van. I made my case. If they wanted old Booner and Junior to bamboozle them into hustling newspapers in the hot sun, they would have to do so without me.

"I'm telling y'all these dudes are busters. They got us looking like clowns," I told the crew.

"Look, they told us it's honest money. Besides, I'm tired of pushing carts outside of Winn-Dixie," fired back Darryl.

We were getting played by two hustlers and no one saw it but me. The nerve of these two old busters to hustle shorties that could have been their grandsons. I wasn't about to drink the Kool-Aid.

"Pull over! If you guys don't pull over, I'll scream for help and tell the police I'm being held hostage," I yelled.

"Seriously, young blood, look around. You're gonna yell for the police in the Beans?" asked Junior.

He had a point. The last time I saw a cop in my neighborhood he was trying to pick up some schoolgirl on her way home.

"Why don't you calm down and hear us out for a minute? Or would you rather we drop you off at the gas station so you can go back to breaking bread with the homeless dudes?" said Booner.

Well, I had no intention of going back there and putting up with Habib's jokes. I didn't want to listen to his speeches on the ills of the hood or his soon approaching jihad, so I decided to stick around. Besides, Booner and Junior seemed like the types who would have harassed me all summer. They didn't need the money. They never made a profit from selling the newspapers. Picking us up in that rusty, squeaky van was their way of saving us from the penitentiary or, at least, slowing down our race to get there. They also hoped we could discover our history through the very product we were peddling.

Back then and even to this day folks in Miami's inner city didn't care too much for the *Miami Herald*. It didn't cover *our* lives. The paper pretty much reported on the day-to-day of the parts of the city that we never saw. Liberty City, Overtown, Opa-locka, and Ghouls would get an occasional headline when some kid got his head blown off. Our paper was the *Miami Times*. A Bahamian dude by the name of Henry Reeves started the paper to cover our issues. On its pages Miami's black history was recorded daily. Junior and Booner took pride in relaying that history.

"You guys know why this paper was started, right?" Booner would say. We had heard it all our lives, but Booner sure gave us his abbreviated version. "The mainstream media took a liking to calling us coons, jigaboos, and whatever other insults they could muster," he said, turning to Junior, who nodded his approval.

"Judging by the likes of how you kids are behaving these days, I can't say I give them any wrong," Junior chimed in.

"Can we get to how we're gonna make this money?" I interrupted. Darryl and O'Sean nodded.

The old men were going to give a rebuttal, but the fact that they had gotten all three of us in van was a start. The civil rights lesson would have to wait.

We were like a street team. We marched throughout the

city armed with newspapers, canvassing all of Twenty-seventh Avenue and Seventh Avenue. Business was especially good in Overtown and Liberty City of course. I ran up to drivers at traffic lights, "Get your *Miami Times!* . . . Get your *Miami Times!*" Most of the drivers were polite. But when we traveled farther south into some of the suburbs like Pinecrest, it was evident that Miami hadn't gotten past its racial demons. King and Malcolm had already died to change things, but down in Miami it seemed folks didn't get the memo. Booner and Junior always had to show officers a permit when we pulled up to an intersection. They let us continue, but they obviously wanted us to sell our papers then get the hell out of *there*.

Elderly white women were especially rude. I would run up to the window to show off the newspaper's headline while they sat in their Volvos. I beamed a broad smile to show off my pearly whites, but they locked their doors and rolled up their windows. In case the power lock didn't work, they jammed their elbow against the door. It was especially amusing to see when those with automatic windows felt their windows weren't going up fast enough. It was as if they saw the grim reaper approaching.

It didn't matter how many days they saw me out there. In their twisted minds, that day could have been the day I was going to maul them to death with a newspaper. Those demons would rise up in me with the fury of Africa and compel me to tomahawk them to death with the *Miami Times*. Picture a ten-year-old bludgeoning good old Martha Stewart to death with the *Wall Street Journal*. That would be a sight for sore eyes. The thing about bigotry that always confuses me is whether the bigot ever realizes how irrational his behavior is. Seriously, you despise a ten-year-old boy selling newspapers for the simple makeup of his DNA? And *they* say that black people have the real issues. Go figure.

Booner would always pull us aside and try to explain the behavior. He knew it offended us. "Guys, some people are always gonna be victims of their own hate. Just pray for them because they're the ones who are really suffering," he would say.

I nodded but he knew I wasn't *listening*. Go save that politically correct speech for the Harlem Boys Choir. Me, Darryl, and O'Sean were kids from the Beans who caught hell upon leaving the womb. Those old ladies looked like they were doing just fine to me in their Volvos and mansions along the bay. I'm sure their kids all graduated from Ivy League schools and were living high on the hog. Hell, their sons and daughters were probably the prosecutors giving out life sentences to young brothers on their first offense. The world isn't fair by any means. I knew Booner meant well, but I wasn't buying it. Save your pie-in-the-sky ideals, old man. In the game of life the good guys finish last, especially in Miami.

The money was good, however. At $.15 a paper, we were guaranteed a $.10 tip. Most days we each sold a hundred papers. That added up to $10. For a ten- or eleven-year-old that was a lot of money. I could go to the flea market and buy a pair of cheap shoes. The Scotch tape I used to cover the holes in my sneakers had worn thin. In the South we had jigga worms. They bore dens in the soles of your feet. Besides, this gig was different from the others. I didn't think of it as a hustle. Booner and Junior made us believe selling those papers was a service to society. We were in the information-exchange business. It was a respectable job. I was proud to be a newspaper courier.

When the day ended, they treated us to dinner. They

took us over to Jumbo's at the corner of Seventh Avenue and Seventy-fifth Street. We laughed and talked about the day while gulping down those spicy morsels. I used to stare at the homeless stragglers who congregated inside. They looked like the world had chewed them up, spit them in an alley, and said go to hell. Nevertheless, the staff was always gracious to them. With our pockets fat and stomachs filled, we headed back to the Beans. My mother enjoyed when I came home and rattled off the crazy events that went on in my day. All that mattered was that I wasn't out robbing and jacking. Also, the job helped us out tremendously. I used the money to buy school clothes for myself and my brothers and sisters.

But it wouldn't be too long before selling the *Miami Times* would fare less profitable than the good green. The herb was making its way to Miami in boatloads and via the friendly skies. Everyone was getting high in the projects. I wanted to reap the benefits.

8

In da Wind

THAT COMMUNIST CAT KARL MARX CALLED RELIGION the "opiate of the people." He was definitely onto something. There is a reason why people in poor countries are so religious. Look at Roman Catholicism in South America. The black church's grip on America's inner cities is legendary. Now don't get me wrong, I consider myself a God-fearing person—with a lot of questions—but God-fearing nonetheless. Most folks wouldn't know God if He was standing right in front of them. For every true servant of God, hundreds more are selling pie in the sky. That's why it's not a coincidence that churches in slums are packed on Sunday morning while hell blazes right outside the front door. In fact, Liberty City has over three hundred churches, and I assure you just as many crack houses. I should know. A lot of my relatives filled them. I guess folks need something to help them escape their harsh realities. For some it's the Holy Ghost, and for others—the ghosts they see high on that good green. Bob Marley isn't the only ambassador sent to us via the Caribbean Sea. Marijuana was a far less honorable one hailing from those same lush tropical islands. It came north from South America as well.

Weed was everywhere in Miami. It was our opium so to speak, a black man's chardonnay. It was so prevalent throughout the city that it wasn't out of the ordinary for the six-o'clock news to fill airtime with a story about some pounds washing up onshore. Pounds of the stuff could literally be found floating along the docks and canals. Young Caribbean cats used to go to the airport to pick up pounds in suitcases shipped by their relatives in Jamaica and beyond. In the Beans and other projects there were no go-to connect for the stuff since it was so much in abundance. Even a few ten-year-olds could cop the stuff, and so we did. I wanted to get paid.

At first the older dudes that were dealing gave me and my friends a couple joints to carry to folks in the neighborhood. Sometimes they gave me as much as an ounce to transport. They noticed I kept my mouth shut and minded my own business. I was in business.

If good old Booner and Junior knew that we were using their van as a drug caravan, they would have skinned us alive. I remember their very first ground rule.

"Now there won't be any funny stuff going on in this van. I know all of you are good boys, no matter what people try to say about your neighborhood," Booner said. That's the ironic thing about life. They were trying to do good by us and the community. If one of those cops who didn't like us selling papers in those rich suburbs wanted a reason to shut down the operation, the marijuana blunts tucked neatly in my tube socks would have given them more than enough reason.

Junior and Booner would have been booked and charged with drug trafficking. Furthermore, they would have been booked for endangering the welfare of kids. All those two God-fearing gentlemen were trying to do was save our sorry-ass lives. We smacked them squarely in the face. But business was good. Damn good.

Kids in those wealthy areas had never been to Liberty City. The closest they ever came to the Beans were the stories they read in the *Miami Herald* or saw on the evening news. To them we were scary little thugs with guns that mirrored hand cannons, and all of our fathers were serving life sentences for armed robbery. It made us superheroes in their eyes. I was always confused as to how they could live in those homes with butlers, nannies, and the latest comic books and still fantasize about our lives. It took me a while to figure it out. The people in those neighborhoods weren't exactly *living* life. Theirs was all scripted. Boredom and emptiness come with a life built on a fairy tale. Seriously, they faced their own sort of hell in that shallow world. Those kids could never say that they actually *achieved* something. They were tied to Daddy's wallet. Mommy and Daddy would buy little Tommy's sanity. When Tommy was caught with the weed he bought from some little nigger from the Beans, he would be sent to therapy. When in fact Tommy just wanted attention, but Daddy was too busy boning his secretary, and that's why Mommy was doing the gardener. Truthfully, myself and Tommy were no different as we were both lost, but he had the best counselors to get his shit straight before heading to Harvard.

Back then, I hadn't come up with such an in-depth analysis. Those crackers wanted a graphic tale of what went down in the Beans, and we were happy to oblige. Of course we added a bit of exaggeration to feed their appetites even more. My stories began in dramatic fashion.

"My daddy ran in the house, tied the robber up, and poured gasoline all over him" would be the lead of one of my classic tall tales. "He dragged him out in the courtyard and lit him on fire for all to see!"

"Wow, that's so cool!" my audience yelled, hanging on every word. Darryl and O'Sean gave hand gestures for emphasis.

"Yeah, but that wasn't the best part. The craziest part was when . . ." I paused. "Can't tell you guys the rest of the story. I'd have to kill you if I do."

For some cash I'd continue.

I myself was taken aback by the scope of my imagination. I would go on and on, all the while taking their cheese. Hell, they were going to use the cheddar on comic books anyhow. Why not put it in our pockets? We needed it more. Furthermore, we sold some of the best weed. Every dope man will tell you his dope is the best. He's like a car salesman that won't let you leave his lot, but my crew did have that good shit.

With $50 we bought five bags of weed. We broke it down, then rolled a hundred $1 joints. We then put it in manila envelopes and stamped it. "Dope Bell" gave you that cool high. It gave the kind of high that gets you floating in the breeze while imagining some half-naked chick is about to do the do on you. "Jack the Ripper" perked you up a bit. "Free Mandela" had you quoting that righteous shit. Any of the three took you to that special place. That place far away from the Beans. I don't think I need to describe the high you got from "Kilimanjaro" and "Criss Cross." The Jamaicans called theirs "7 Cents."

Like I said earlier, we didn't have one particular connect, but Jean at Winn-Dixie hooked us up well. Yeah, he was a grimy bastard. But I can't blame the man. He had a wife and three kids back in Port-au-Prince he was supporting. It worked out well. Alongside your meat and vegetables you could get high on that magic-carpet ride.

We took to buying the regular toys and other stuff ten-year-olds would have purchased with the newfound wealth. Music. Sneakers. Comics.

Jean advised us to put a little bit away for a rainy day, but at that age, who was listening? It might sound far-fetched that a crew of ten-year-olds had their own weed-selling operation, but this was Miami. We weren't special. Most youngsters growing up in the hood back then sold *something*. My city is a port where things come in and we export it to the rest of America. It was only fitting for a couple of youngsters to join in on the hustle. From rolling joints I learned how to make a quick flip and gamble.

The main part of any hustle is being able to sell yourself. Having the slickest tongue will get you far with the buyers. Having the slickest and wittiest tongue will get you far in life period. It's no different in gambling. Being able to call another person's bluff while keeping him in the dark is the name of the game. So I tried my hand at the crap game. At first those older dudes wouldn't let me in on the game. Eventually I gassed their heads up so much I forced them to let me in. I played possum. They were unaware I had watched them for months, hoping to get in and take their pesos. Tank was especially determined to take my cash. "Let his young ass join in on the game," he told the other dudes. "Don't go home crying to your mama when you lose all your lunch money, chump."

That was the opening I needed. In the streets it's always good to let the other man underestimate you. That way he shows his hand and goes in foolhardy while you keep your biggest weapons heavily guarded until he's spent his. It's kind of like a boxer who fights defensive for eleven rounds then unleashes his uppercut in the twelfth. I let Tank kick my ass for at least five hands, then I started cleaning up. As I collected his cash, I won over the crowd. "Y'all check this out! Tank's getting wiped out by the young-un!" someone shouted. "The jit's cleaning him out of his last dime!"

People came running up from the basketball court. Folks were cheering me on. My crew was the loudest. But I forgot to not let my ego get my ass killed.

Tank's name was self-explanatory. He was stuck on steroids or something. His testosterone was on overdrive. His size was only rivaled by his ego. No one fucked with Tank. I guess everyone who couldn't dare insult Tank was using me as an avenue to do just that. I soaked it in.

"You're not talking now, are you? What happened? Oh, you're losing all your money. Sorry, I forgot," I taunted. I was signing my death warrant wide-eyed.

"Shut your young ass up," warned Tank.

"Or what?" It's so easy to get carried away with everyone cheering you on. Tank gave me a chance and I didn't take it. Looking back, I think he respected me because no one in the

Beans dared stand up to him. They were smart. In five seconds, I was staring square-eyed down the barrel of his pistol.

"Come on, Tank? How you gonna pull a gun on a shorty?" someone asked.

"Nah, he grown. He grown enough to disrespect me in my own motherfucking projects." Tank looked like a man possessed.

My heart raced. I was scared shitless. Standing there, with that gun to my forehead, I lost all sense of reality. In seconds my life could be over. I didn't even get to dive into some panties yet. Just a minute ago I thought this was all a game, just some honest fun. Tank would get angry, but we'll laugh at it later over a happy meal.

"Say something, motherfucker! I bet I'll leave your brains all over this pavement," he yelled.

How did I get here? If you've ever had a gun pulled on you, you know that feeling of powerlessness. All control is gone. Your life is hanging upon the whim of one simple squeeze of the trigger. By now the crowd had dissipated. Only Darryl and O'Sean were left. My crew had heart. But the only thing that could save me now was a moment of sanity in Tank's crazed mind. Did he realize he had a pistol pressed against the skull of a ten-year-old in broad daylight? Oh, I forgot. The cops patrolling Liberty City had already petitioned to get their hours reduced. The police chief felt it was wiser to increase the squad in areas where the residents seemed more genetically predisposed to live longer.

I didn't flinch. I squeezed my fists tight. I was ready. I was scared, but what good was it going to do to piss my pants and beg old Tank to let me go? If he was going to shoot me, I'd rather Pearl didn't find me lying out on the concrete with my shorts soaked. Tank had killed before. I would just be another notch on his belt. I closed my eyes.

"Empty your pockets," Tank demanded.

I gave him the couple hundred bucks I had. Darryl handed over the envelope with the remaining joints we hadn't sold.

"You little fuck niggas got Jack the Ripper!?" Tank exclaimed. "How y'all got your hands on this good shit?"

O'Sean blurted out, "Oh, we got it from—"

"Shut your ass up!" Tank interrupted.

I thought about all the things I didn't and would never get to do. They were all a blur now. Then, I felt the pistol's barrel drop from my head.

"I ain't gonna kill you, shorty," Tank said. "You a wild little nigga that got heart. But if you ever disrespect me again, I'll blow your fucking head off."

I stood there and watched him walk away. Tank took something away from me that day. In those two minutes or so my childhood faded. I left it there on the curb in the Beans. It wasn't the last time I would have a gun pulled on me. It was the only time I wasn't prepared to shoot back.

These were the growing pains of a kid raised in the Beans.

My crew looked at me. I knew they depended on me. When I said ride, we rode. So I did what any other young hustler on the come-up would do. I got a gun.

9

Ninety-nine Problems

MOST FOLKS IN THE HOOD IN MIAMI CARRIED FIRE. I just hadn't been in a situation yet to need a pistol myself. Even Pearl kept a .22. I'll never forget the day I came home and she had it pointed at some old dude who was loitering around our apartment trying to flirt with my sister. Teenage girls in the suburbs have slumber parties and talk about their first crush. Jewish families throw bat mitzvahs to usher in their daughters' approaching womanhood. Wealthy Hispanic girls have quinceañera. In the Beans, burgeoning curves meant you became prey for old, perverted bastards that raped chicks under the bleachers adjacent to the basketball court. Pearl wasn't having it.

"I swear, if you come at my girls again, you won't have a johnson to wave at them!" she yelled. "I'll shoot it off!"

That pervert ran dizzy through the courtyard. Having been taken advantage of by men her entire life, Pearl refused to see her daughters fall victim to the same abuse. I asked her where she got the fire from.

"None of your damn business! You think you're grown now? Don't ever let me see you with a gun in my house."

But news traveled fast in the Beans. Folks knew if you needed a pistol, Jo Jo over in the Blueberries was the person to go see. His father was locked up in federal prison for gun smuggling. Jo Jo was carrying on the family business. The dude's apartment was stocked like the National Guard armory. Jo Jo wasn't older than fifteen, but he lived alone with his two younger sisters. He gave his neighbor some money to pretend to be his mom when the child services people came snooping around. Like I said earlier, everyone had a side hustle. When I knocked on his door later that week, he wasn't particularly inviting.

"What they do?" asked Jo Jo.

I peeked into the peephole. "Your cousin Ray told me to come see you about that fire."

"Bruh, I don't have no cousin named Ray, and the only fire I know is the one burning in the Everglades. So if you ain't with the Miami-Dade fire department come to inspect my apartment, you need to keep it moving!"

I pulled out a $100 bill and slid it under the door.

The door cracked. Jo Jo looked me up and down and shook his head. "Damn, you ain't nothing but a little nigga."

I stepped in. His sisters were playing with a dollhouse on the floor. Jo Jo waved me into his bedroom closet. The kid's closet looked like Iwo Jima. He had assault rifles, semiautomatics, silencers, even a grenade.

"Damn, bruh, how you got all—"

"Hold up, my nigga," replied Jo Jo. "First and foremost, you don't ask no questions in relations to another nigga's trade. You should know that. I know your old boy's an OG. He's locked up with my pops in the Feds."

I gazed at the floor. I would inevitably have to have that conversation, but right now I wanted a hand cannon. I wanted a pistol that could fire a bullet the size of Texas into Tank's chest.

Jo Jo brought out a chrome .38 with a black handle. It glittered all over when the closet light shone on it. It now belonged to me. Jo Jo tucked the $100 in a shoebox. "If your young ass gets arrested, they don't know where you got the fire from," he said sternly.

I nodded, then hit the courtyard. It was on. I rounded up my crew, who were on the basketball court shooting hoops. I showed off the chrome beauty tucked in my shorts. I was becoming a man. I couldn't wait to find Tank.

I got your little fuck nigga.

My blood boiled over. The adrenaline rush of the streets is addictive. You can't get enough of the drama while you're spiraling down a dead end.

At that moment all I could think about was firing a full clip into Tank so folks would know not to mess with me. If you began it, I would sure as hell finish it. My crew looked at me as if they knew something I didn't. O'Sean finally blurted it out.

"Tank got shot."

"Yeah, somebody capped his ass," said Darryl.

This wasn't a game after all. In the Beans, lives evaporated like mud puddles on a hot summer's day. I felt a twinge of sorrow for Tank. Just minutes ago I was sure I wanted to be the one to end his life. That's the messed-up thing about being raised in a jungle. You start acting like an animal. Did I really want Tank's life to end? *Of course not.* A ten-year-old doesn't know the true consequences of death.

Tank was gone.

There could be no saying I'm sorry to his parents or maybe the girl and child he left behind. In the hood things happen in a blur. You race through life in a fog of anger and resentment. Most murders aren't thought out or planned. Sometimes someone just gets scared or angry and a body is left cold and crumpled on the concrete. The coroner's office marks your sorry ass off as John Doe.

I'm sure Tank had it coming. He had put many dudes to sleep in his mere eighteen years on the planet. But no one wins when someone gets killed. One brother is trapped below six feet of dirt and worms, and the other's in a six-by-nine-foot cell.

They say Tank ran up on some dudes who had just moved to the Beans from Scott Carver projects. A lot of violence occurs when people are displaced from one project to another. The new crew is usually trying to move in on drug turf, forcing the resident crew to defend it. Tank lost that fight.

"Shit, he had it coming," I boasted, concealing my inner anguish over his death. "He's lucky they got to him first."

My crew looked at one another. They understood that Maurice was going to be a force to be reckoned with. We weren't taking any shit from anyone. When I walked through the hood, something was different. The means by which you earn stripes in the hood is so warped it's downright insane.

I got props for not begging for my life when Tank put his pistol to my head. It made Maurice a "stone-cold motherfucker."

I had balls . . . big ones. My clientele increased. It was known throughout the Beans, Blueberries, and Green Machine that my crew had the weed to get you to that special place. You know, the place where you forgot your rent is overdue and they're about to turn off the lights. Hell, I was the go-to guy to get high. News surely does travel fast in the hood.

10

Boy

To say I didn't like school would be an understatement. I hated the place. I didn't see the sense. No one in the Beans or anyone I knew for that matter had used school to gain any respectability in life. As far as I saw it, the teachers drove Pintos. Why go to college to earn a degree if it landed you square back in the hood teaching my sorry ass?

Honestly, I and the other kids at Charles Drew Middle appeared to be lost causes. Most of us would either get locked up or die in the Beans. The school itself was as much as part of our neighborhood as the crummy apartments. Folks raised in Liberty Square went to Charles Drew. It was your typical middle school in any inner-city neighborhood. It was the kind of school where a majority of the teachers showed up to get a check, the folks who at the last minute figured their grades weren't good enough to get them into law school or medical school. Now, there were and still always are some educators in inner-city public schools who fight tooth and nail for kids society has given up on. The sad truth is such teachers get lost in the shuffle amid the mayhem . . . usually caused by students such as yours truly.

I went to Drew to sell weed. During lunch and PE, I had the kids coming in and out of the boys' bathroom while my crew kept guard. Even a teacher or two were getting blown on my supply. Don't act surprised. You guys really think your English teacher didn't puff on the good green on his or her lunch break? Of course they did. However, all good things do come to an end.

Kids like me were conveniently served detention when the superintendent arrived for his routine walk-through. One knucklehead hall monitor was onto me. Every school always has one. He has to be the exception. That student is the kid the principal puts in charge of campus tours. At Drew his name was Timothy.

Timothy was a buster. If not for his bifocals, I would have sucker punched him in the face months before. But knocking out some herb wouldn't have been good for my street cred. He got me good though. The dude never spoke to me, so I should have known something was up when he came running up to me at lunchtime one Friday.

Fridays were when I usually tried to stack as much cheese as I could. Our crew went to the skating rink on the weekends. I had to get the freshest kicks. I was down to my last dollar joint when he ran up to me.

"Hey, I heard you got that head buster," I remember him saying, or something to that effect.

"I don't know what you're talking about, bruh," I replied.

Good old Timmy was persistent. He pulled out $20. My better judgment should have seen the trap miles away, but I was a sucker for lady green. I motioned him to the bathroom, then opened the toilet dispenser where I stashed my supply.

Timmy's eyes lit up. I smirked. I'm sure he was impressed with my resourcefulness. He may have been making straight A's in the classroom, but I was a young Einstein on the street. *I wasn't that bright.* I gave the school janitor a few bucks to keep it a secret.

In seconds, those school police officers descended on me like a pack of wolves.

It wasn't even the weed I got booked for. When I opened the dispenser, it wasn't there. I guess someone treated himself to a free high. The look on those cops' faces was worth its weight in gold. I laughed until one yanked me up against the wall. If he could have clubbed me with the baton, I'm sure he would have. They searched my backpack. Inside, they found my gun wrapped in my gym shorts.

Busted. My first arrest. I was hauled down to the Miami-Dade Juvenile Detention Center, but they couldn't book me because I was too young.

Your first time in handcuffs is the most painful to grasp. The look on your mother's face fills you with regret for causing her such pain. After some scolding, you promise to do better but the damage is done. You've begun your lifelong love affair with shackles and bars. It's a matrimony whose vows are literally etched in "till death do us part." You're trapped.

I'll say this to every prosecutor, district attorney, public defender, and judge in America: Your juvenile justice system is bullshit. It's designed to send thousands of black and Hispanic kids down an unforgiving path to a life of revolving prison doors. Most of these officials wouldn't have jobs if they implemented measures to address the root of the problem. In no way can they justify putting an eleven-year-old in handcuffs.

The harsh truth is that, in the eyes of the powers that be, a life in the Beans isn't worth as much as one from Coral Gables. Kids in those posh private schools are up to the same mayhem. The only difference is that, instead of getting sent to juvie, they're sent to therapists and counselors. Why pay to figure out the cause of little Maurice's demons?

Shit, let's lock this little nigger up before he grows into a real problem. If we cage him up early, he won't be able to kill us all.

In Miami-Dade public schools alone there's an average of two thousand arrests annually. About half of those arrested are black students. The Miami-Dade Juvenile Detention Center holds on average twelve thousand kids. Imagine all that money going to high-priced security and correctional officers' pockets instead of going toward a rec center of some sort in the Beans. Some of it could go to extra lighting on the basketball court or maybe a security guard so the little brothers could shoot hoops without the hookers turning tricks under the bleachers. They'd rather spend that cheese on more police. I never understood why officials think punishment as opposed to prevention will decrease the crime rate. I wasn't selling weed or toting a pistol because I liked the fancier things. Yeah, maybe I bought a sneaker here and there, but that cash kept the lights on in my mother's crib. She didn't know it of course. Pearl wouldn't have stood for her kids' school clothes being bought with dope money.

When she picked me up that Friday, Pearl's stare burned right through me. It beamed with a sense of hopelessness. She was fighting a losing battle. The stacks were piled against her. The streets were stealing her firstborn son. The silence on the bus ride home was deafening. Sometimes the unspoken message in silence booms louder than a drum. That day it busted my eardrum.

You're gonna be a fuckup like every other sorry nigger in these projects.

Sadly enough, I was going into the fire eyes wide-open. No one gave a damn anyway. When we reached the door, Pearl snapped. The blow to the back of my head knocked me down cold on the doorstep. Darryl and O'Sean, who were chilling in the courtyard, saw the whole thing.

"Damn, Maurice just got smacked!" Darryl yelled.

"If y'all don't want to catch some of what he's about to get, I'd advise y'all to go home," my mother yelled.

All I saw was the dust kicked up from Darryl's and O'Sean's sneakers. They ran faster than the devil caught outside a Baptist church on Palm Sunday.

"What the hell you doing with a gun in the schoolhouse?" my mother snapped. "Lord, sweet Jesus, I'm about to catch a case on this boy."

I had two options. I could tell the truth, that I really wasn't working extra hours with Booner and Junior. The money I used to buy my new PE shorts really came from the bags of weed I'd been stashing in the vent above the sink in the bathroom. I would have been justified. I got tired of the food-stamp jokes. I got tired of being teased at school and having the teachers call me and my siblings nappy-headed welfare cases. Somebody had to take up where none of Pearl's baby fathers did. How could you expect an eleven-year-old to play man of the house and make the best decisions? *Pearl we got dealt a fucked-up hand and I got a pistol because the life I'm about to embark on calls for it.* I went with option number two.

"I don't know. I forgot my backpack in the classroom all day. Someone must have stashed it in my bag when I wasn't looking."

The "it wasn't me" worked in the movies. So why shouldn't it work for me?

"Boy, you got one more chance to tell me the truth. I really think you want the devil to rise up out of me. I'm trying real hard, Maurice."

"I told you I don't know how it got there."

It was time for an ass-whupping. I knew the drill. I went outside to the ficus tree in the courtyard and broke off the skinniest branch. My mother shredded the branches' smaller limbs as she continued her interrogation. I didn't budge. Hell, a sound whupping was better than the beating I would have got if I told her the truth. Pearl liked Booner and Junior. Everyone in the hood did. They were well respected. When my mother thought I was out with them selling newspapers, I was selling weed. I got tired of those white ladies jamming their car doors on me. I took a deep breath and closed my eyes.

My screams rang out through the neighborhood. It always seemed like everyone was home when you got a whipping. Kids peeked outside their windows. Some of the older folks cheered her on.

"That's right, sister! Spare the rod, spoil the child!" the chants began. "You got to beat the devil out the young-uns these days!"

I don't know about elsewhere, but in the South black folks take whippings seriously. It's a time-honored tradition. You would think it's Mardi Gras when black folks spank their kids. They get real into it, as if they are possessed. Don't think about not crying either. If I played tough guy, my mother spanked me even harder.

"Maurice, you know I got better things to do than come down to that schoolhouse and deal with your foolishness!" Pearl yelled as she slammed that branch against my rear end. Black spankings must look like child abuse to the civilized world I'm sure, but kids in the hood know that the pain their parents are trying to save them from bruises far more severely. It's why black folks spank their kids. A mistake in the hood could cost you your life. Black parents whip their kids out of fear. It's the horror that comes with seeing other kids carried off to prison or draped in white sheets. The consequences are too great in Anyhood, USA. Time out doesn't send a clear enough message.

Pearl's anger subsided into tears. She dropped the branch and grabbed me. She squeezed me close to her chest. I felt the tears falling onto me.

"Mommy, please don't cry. I won't do it again. I promise," I said, trying to console her.

"I can't lose you, Maurice. Please, I can't lose you, baby," she sobbed. "Next they'll call me to identify your body."

I wiped my mother's tears. The only thing that had kept the streets from devouring me whole thus far was the fear of disappointing her. We were dealt a shitty hand indeed, starring in a bad episode of *This is Your Life*. The harsh reality was that her tears were wasted. The only thing I regretted was getting caught. Most burgeoning crooks can relate. The guys breaking down in those interrogation rooms on the show *The First 48* aren't sobbing because they feel remorse. They're mad they were dumb enough to get caught.

If only I had dumped the body in the river instead of the lake.

It's scary, but it's been proven that people have to be reached on a personal level to save them from becoming heartless. Scared straight doesn't work. If one of those steroid-pumping enforcers had screamed at me as a troubled kid on *Maury*, I would have sucker punched him. I would have reacted that way because I felt disrespected. Those scare tactics don't work on kids who have been yelled and screamed at all their lives. The counselor becomes just another bully trying to humiliate them.

11

Gangsta

I WAS EXPELLED FROM CHARLES DREW THE FOLLOWING week. My numerous absences and alleged dope dealing was reason enough to get me up out of there. I was looking forward to attending another school and starting off fresh. For the time being, I adhered to the wishes of my mother and school counselor. They sent me to Brownsville Middle; in weeks, trouble struck again.

Some people enjoy getting a rise out of the person in the group who sticks out. People target the individual who seems up for a good challenge. I was always an aggressive dude. Like Pearl, if you wanted a war, I would bring the grenade, rocket launcher, and cannon. Come on with it. As hard as I tried to keep that internal ticking bomb from going off, someone had to force the explosion.

At Brownsville, his name was Mr. Tuttle.

Tuttle was the music teacher. No one ever took his class seriously. We sat there staring off into space, daydreaming, and waited for the bell to ring. I think Tuttle knew his class was the last pain in the ass for everyone and reveled in it. The fat bastard made us sit there until the very last minute. I'm sure everyone had such a class.

"Come on, everybody, on one again," Tuttle would say. "Let's go, and one and two and three . . ."

As much as we hated his anal ways, we disliked even more the way he accentuated his *T*'s. Let me explain. The only sound that rivaled the flamboyant trumpets in that band room was Tuttle's voice. He was of that persuasion. I don't discriminate against anyone's choice for love and affection. I frankly don't give a damn if a dude has a certain curve in his step, if you know what I mean. That's the problem with folks. People always try to lash out against those who are different. Go clean the bones hiding in your closet before you throw a stone at your neighbor. I'm not here to judge. Diversity makes the world a better place. The best salad has a wide array of fruits and vegetables. One of my sisters is more of a dude than I am, and I love her to death.

But back then folks who were of an alternative sexual orientation had it rough. They were bashed. We've come a long way since those days as society has learned to accept folks for who they are. However, try explaining to a class of middle schoolers in Liberty City why their music teacher had a certain sway to his swag. . . . You get the point. Looking back, I think Tuttle tried to send a message.

His flamboyance was beyond anything in the ordinary. The guy used to hit high notes. A typical class entailed sitting through soprano ballads. The more we twisted and turned in our seats, the more Tuttle sashayed across the room. I can't blame the guy for being bold in his sexuality. When a person is accustomed to being attacked, his natural defense is to put up a front. I guess Tuttle was going to force people to accept him whether they liked it or not.

He chose me as his sounding board.

I said it before and I'll say it again. I've always been suspect. Imagine going to a comedy show with a sellout crowd. The comedian readies his routine that begins with his making fun of someone in the audience. Who does he put the spotlight on? Maurice Young.

About ten minutes were left in the class when Tuttle turned the spotlight on me. I usually sat in the back, where I could stay off the teacher's radar. I noticed Tuttle had grown fond of calling on me when he saw I wasn't paying attention. I was already having a bad day as I was short on my re-up money to buy more weed, which meant I would be spending the evening gambling in the Beans.

"Mr. Young, come to the board," Tuttle told me. "Come on, hurry up. We don't have all day."

"Sorry, I don't know the notes," I replied.

I wasn't getting off the hook that easy.

"I'm not going to repeat myself. No one is leaving until you come to the chalkboard," insisted Tuttle. "I said move it!"

I gazed at the floor. From the corners of my eyes I caught a glimpse of my classmates. I knew if I did what Tuttle demanded, I'd be viewed as a sucker. Worse, it may have sanctioned me as his bitch. Kids in middle school can be harsh. I got up and shuffled toward the board. The taunting ensued.

"You gonna let that punk talk to you like that?" someone whispered. "Told y'all he ain't hard," another kid chimed in.

A million thoughts raced through my mind. I was just expelled from Charles Drew less than two months before. If not for my lack of interest, I could have gotten straight A's. In fact, I don't think I was being challenged. A bell rang in my head. Obeying Tuttle would most definitely strip me of my manhood. I couldn't let that happen. It meant every other kid in the Beans who thought he was tough would try me. Then I would definitely have to shoot someone. I turned around. I felt a hand grab my shirt collar. I wasn't the only one trying to assert my manhood. Tuttle was apparently trying to do the same. I gazed at the lead pipe positioned at the base of the classroom door to keep it ajar.

"Let go of me!" I yelled.

"And if I don't, what the hell are you gonna do?" Tuttle fired back.

The sad truth is I never disliked Tuttle. We had something in common. I never fitted in anywhere either. Like Tuttle, I was a misfit. I've always been determined to do my own thing regardless of the status quo. If the crowd went left, I bolted right. At that moment my rebellious DNA led me to the pipe.

In seconds Tuttle was laid out on the classroom floor. I hit him squarely upside his head. I needed my manhood more than Tuttle did his. My hustling depended on it. I held the lead pipe over him as if I was the HNIC. He pleaded and covered his face as I taunted him. The class cheered. Minutes later I was in handcuffs. Again.

This time the cuffs weren't so painful. I could not have cared less about going back down to the detention center to be processed. Tuttle got what was coming to him. He tried me. On the way down to the center the officer gave me the usual lecture about the dangers that come with the path I was heading down. I didn't give a damn. I was ready to travel that rocky road. Besides, inside those fenced walls I got time to think. No one came to get me for a week or so. By now folks in my life were getting fed up.

When my mother finally came to get me, she didn't give a speech. She didn't even whup my ass. That's when you know you're *losing*. When folks are hard on you, it's because they care. Start worrying when you become invisible. I couldn't blame Pearl. She had ten other kids to worry about. If Maurice wanted to throw his life away, why waste energy on him? In the hood single mothers play lotto. They look at their kids. Chances are one of their sons will most likely die from a gunshot not too far from their doorstep. Another will inevitably be hauled off to state prison. If fate felt sorry for her, one son would stay at home, serve burgers for a living, and raise his family in that cramped apartment. At least he'll be alive.

She hit the jackpot if one son went to college. The scene from the movie *Boyz N the Hood* depicted it well. Ricky's mother fainted when he got shot. Doughboy was left, but who cared. Those are the slots played by mothers in the Beans and other projects throughout the United States. I wasn't exactly Doughboy. I was the kid Pearl knew had potential, but was throwing it away. So she focused her attention on her other kids. I was expelled again.

I took to running the streets. The time out of the classroom while educators sought a suitable alternative for me left me with hours to dedicate to hustling. My crew had the Beans smoking like a chimney. Word had spread that my weed was straight from the mountains of Herbland, Jamaica, the place where every weed head dreams about going to. It's where a half-naked big-butt vixen rolls your blunts while another massages your back. Well, I know it's a stretch. But a place like that would definitely be dope.

By the time school officials found an alternative program for me to attend, I was totally dedicated to pushing my product. Wherever they sent me I was determined to make my cash cow. They chose Jan Mann.

Jan Mann Opportunity School was a hustler's dream. Let's just say it was like literally taking candy from a baby. Teachers at regular public schools in the hood don't give a damn, so try doing a survey on morale at the alternative programs. The American public school system has a hierarchy. Take an educated guess on where alternative programs fall on that totem poll? If you answered at the bottom, you hit the mark.

Some teachers in those crap shoots are dedicated to making a difference in the lives of those little aspiring felons, but they never get enough credit. The system is broken from the top down, but the teacher in there who's being subjected to threats and all sorts of other harm always gets the blame for failure. I actually used to feel sorry for some of the teachers at Jan Mann. How could society expect them to play the role of teacher, counselor, parent, and protector? Their backs were against the wall. It was a stressful place for kids and educators alike. So I did what any other concerned student would do to lighten the load. I got folks high as a kite.

At Jan Mann, who was going to tell? The school sits in the heart of Opa-locka, where shots from the Blues projects ring out daily. It wasn't unusual for a shoot-out from the projects to spill out into the school. Officials would have to lock it down while cops chased the shooter through our campus. The area known as the Triangle was put on the map as the most violent zip code in America. Former mayor Robert Ingram barricaded the neighborhood with a triangle-shaped fence to contain the area's violence. He actually had to cage those folks in.

Given that information about Jan Mann's locale, do you really think the school's staff was worried about Maurice Young's weed supply? I turned that place into the set from the movie *Half Baked*. I had the general run of Jan Mann. While security was busy chasing down *real* crooks, yours truly flooded the halls with the good green.

At lunchtime I served some of the dudes from the neighborhood. I gave one of the security guards a couple dollars so he could wave me through the metal detectors. Of course I still carried my fire. A dope boy's pistol is like a preacher's Bible. He should never leave home without it. But like any young, foolhardy kid, I got overconfident. I got ahead of myself. The pickings were just too easy at Jan Mann. I decided to start bringing in larger quantities of my supply. The idea was to start employing runners. A couple of the cats in the Blues wanted in.

I knew I could use the help to grow my business, even though my better judgment should have told me that in any enterprise one should keep his profits within reason. Anything beyond a quick flip leaves one swimming with the sharks. Up until then Darryl and O'Sean were the only dudes I broke bread with. We trusted each other. I let foolhardiness get the best of me and started outsourcing my supply to dudes I didn't know who could get my product outside the walls of Jan Mann. The extra help meant I needed extra weight.

"Seventy-five bags of marijuana?!" The look on that judge's face when they hauled me into juvenile court for the third time that year was classic. "Somebody explain to me how a twelve-year-old manages to get seventy-five bags of marijuana into a public institution of learning?"

School officials shook their heads in embarrassment. I was quite proud of myself. I was willing to give the judge the break-down on exactly how I did it, minus snitching on my cohorts of course. Even back then, I got a rush from giving the law my ass to kiss. They were the ones who had left us fucked-up and broke in the Beans. That judge wanted to condemn those poor teach-ers for my bullshit? They weren't the problem. Hell, all he had to do was lock me up. That wasn't any skin off his back. Those teachers had to go back to Jan Mann and convince the one or two kids in there who really wanted to turn a corner that their school wasn't a joke. They had to explain that the school wasn't just some garbage bin where the Miami-Dade public school system dumped their trash.

Looking back, I didn't realize just how many problems I caused. That's the thing about living in a world in which we're all connected. Research even proves that babies born in the same nursery absorb each other's pain. When one starts to cry, the others start wailing as well. I don't care if it's a hard pill to swallow. You're responsible to someone. People can't just go around pissing wherever they want. It will stink. Your actions af-fect the lives of others. The superintendent's office launched an investigation. A public school's funding depends on the success rate of its students. Grants, loans, new computers, and all that were decided on how well the kids are doing. They preach that every kid in America has a right to a free education. It's a bunch of politically correct bullshit. In much the same way America's civil liberties are designed to benefit some and leave out others, so is the public school system. Keeping the Maurice Youngs in school directly lowered success rates and indirectly decreased the cash flow. Don't get it twisted. In America every decision ultimately revolves around the dollar bill. It's why the previous two schools were so eager to get me out of there. *You're fucking up our money, young blood.* It wasn't personal. I can't even blame them. Some kids attend school to learn. I didn't.

"You have anything to say for yourself, Mr. Young," the judge asked.

First off, I think the American juvenile justice system is all bullshit. I think your laws are bullshit. If I could, I would come up there and smack the toupee off your cracker head. It's like you guys get off on locking up young niggas instead of giving opportunities. You don't think I'd rather watch cartoons than sell weed on the corner all day? Fuck you, Your Honor. Kiss my black ass.

That's what I wanted to say, but I was fresh, not stupid. Standing there in my oversize, orange jailhouse jumpsuit, shackled from head to toe, my world was shrinking. The windows of possibilities for Maurice Young were closing. My public defender sat next to me in a world of her own. She probably graduated with a subpar GPA from the University of Miami's law school and passed the bar exam by a thread. Now she was stuck defending a kid on a direct path to death or the chain gang. She couldn't wait for the arraignment to end.

The judge gave a good speech: "It always tugs at me that young men such as yourself never realize what you're doing to yourself and those that love you until it's too late. Every day I come into this courtroom and see lives being thrown away."

Sighs echoed throughout the room. The older dudes waiting on their arraignment had heard it all before. They yawned and stared off into space. You always know who just caught their first case. He's the dude all dressed in his Sunday best. He's talking his lawyer's ear off. The seasoned cats stretch their feet out and lounge until the bailiff motions them to the bench.

"Is there a guardian present with your defendant?" the judge asked my public defender.

"No, we were unable to reach Ms. Brockington after several attempts. Her phone seemed to be disconnected and there was no place of employment listed for her," my lawyer replied.

"Figures." The judge shook his head.

They carried me through the steel door that led to the corridor behind the judge's seat. In the long, winding hallway kids sat on an iron bench before they were called in. If a guardian came, the kid was taken back there to be processed for release. The Miami-Dade Juvenile Detention Center was merely an adult prison with children in cages. You would assume a facility that houses kids ages eleven to eighteen would be more suited for adolescents, but there are no classification mandates there. A kid charged with a minor offense could end up sharing a cell with a killer.

The main difference between the center and adult prison was that we attended class. We sat in open spaces called mods. With no chalkboards, the teachers got creative when giving the lesson plan. They tried hard to make the best of a bad situation. Class was routinely interrupted when the buzzer sounded.

It meant a classmate was up for arraignment. The steel door opened and a correctional officer stepped in.

"Inmate twenty-nine, you're up!" he would yell.

"Good luck, homey," a classmate would say. We shared daps when the kid walked by. He was thoroughly searched before exiting. As you can imagine, it was hard to focus on textbooks with your fate hanging in the balance. Across the yard, in the girls' dorms, things weren't much different besides some larger mirrors in the bathrooms. After class we retired to our six-by-nine-foot cells.

The first time Pearl left me in there, I knew she was trying to teach me a lesson. This time around was different. The days got longer. When the buzzer to the steel door finally rang and my number was called, I was relieved. I had stayed in that dungeon for about three weeks. I couldn't wait to get home.

12

Straight Up

PEARL DIDN'T COME TO GET ME. MY UNCLE STOOD outside his Cadillac, which was all tricked out. It was drenched in more chrome than Cinderella's slippers. He was a longtime hustler, the kind that didn't take kindly to busters. I was confused. It wasn't that I minded seeing him, but I expected my mother.

"What's up, young blood?" he asked. "I see you're holding down fort like a young G." My father was locked up in federal prison on drug-trafficking charges, so my uncle pretended he was him to come get me. It hit me. I knew why Pearl didn't come to get me. Remember what I said earlier about a person's actions and the domino effect it caused? When we got to the Beans, Ms. Ridley was inside my apartment trying to console my mother. Pearl was on her knees sobbing.

In the projects if a kid caused trouble, the welfare folks could evict the family. The memo to single mothers was written in clear, straightforward language:

All you had to do was lie on your back all these years and get knocked up by deadbeat dudes. We covered the tab. The least you can do is keep those little niggers tame. Tie them with a leash if you have to. If you can't manage to do that, we're taking back the freebies and kicking your ass out.

Ms. Ridley looked up at me. "Maurice, I know you've been playing man of the house."

"Bullshit! This is bullshit!" I shouted.

"Boy, I already told you about using foul language around me," my mother warned.

Life is ironic, I guess. It brought me back to that desert, the one that hope dragged me out in the middle of. I couldn't win for trying. I was on those streets hustling, trying to make home a happy place. I made sure my younger siblings wouldn't have to take those risks. I chalked it up for what it was. My brothers had some change to go on a field trip. They wouldn't have to be the subject of everyone's jokes. If I ended up dead or in jail, they could use the couple dollars I had stashed up in the vent.

Now the system was telling me the means by which I used to escape the cage they put me in was close to uprooting my family. My uncle nodded. The inevitable was about to happen.

"You have to move," said Ms. Ridley.

Reality hit me. I had grown used to stepping in the shoes left vacated by my father, but I was a child, no doubt. I couldn't let my brothers and sisters be split up. That crummy apartment in the Beans wasn't much, but it was Pearl's home. I packed my things before heading south to stay at my father's house.

His dope slinging, pimping, and numbers running had already made him a household name in the hood. He was one of the OGs in Miami who had noticed early what was happening across the bridge on Miami Beach.

While we scraped by in Liberty City on petty hustling, high-rises were sprouting along Ocean Drive. Benzes and BMWs cruised the strip. Snowbirds flew south during the winter to soak it all in. I guess it was what people would call paradise. In the *other* Miami a couple of hustlers were getting rich off the *white girl*.

13

Snowin' in Miami

EVERY AMERICAN CITY HAS ITS CLAIM TO FAME, HOW-
ever honorable or messed up it may be. New York's pizza is to
die for. I'd like to bone my share of L.A. actresses. Even thug-
ass Philly got cheesesteak. Miami has cocaine. The white girl.
Blow. Bricks. Lace. Pies. Birds. Whatever folks want to call it,
the powder was ours before it lit the rest of America on fire. So
every time you see a dazed addict in your locale, or a cracked-
out hooker peeking from behind a lamppost, credit Miami. It's
funny how death can dwell in the most idyllic of places. There's
blood on the hands of my city. We're drenched in buckets. I
wonder if tourists think about that historical fact when they
come to South Beach. I wonder if they know the ghosts of the

runners, hit men, addicts, and jack boys roam amid those high-rises that tower over Biscayne Bay.

When the powder arrived from Colombia, it caused a blizzard in Miami. Everyone went dancing in the snow. By the time I was five, the Colombian and Cuban dope kings were in an all-out war. Seriously, Miami's streets mirrored some cowboy-and-Indian Wild Wild West shit. Strangely enough though, South Beach was a sleepy little retirement spot. Its couple of mobsters from the old school were no match for the Colombians. As I mentioned earlier, Latin American and Caribbean cats are cut from a different cloth. They don't bow down to anyone, but they knew they were on unfamiliar turf. Picture some Colombian cats crashing some ritzy party down on South Beach with a bunch of white doctors, lawyers, bankers, and other professionals. They would have stuck out like sore thumbs. Remember, these were the days when the city was primarily white or black. I already told you where the black folks were.

In Miami's cutthroat underbelly it was easy to find some opportunistic white dudes to push the powder. Enter Mickey Mundey and Jim Roberts. They were typical all-American cats bent on looting and plundering. Miami always attracts those types to this very day. They got in good with some Colombians who were itching to get their dope to America. Mickey and Jim fit the part. In our hood we heard the stories about those dudes long before the world got a glimpse of the mayhem in that movie *Cocaine Cowboys*. I'm surprised it took so long for some filmmakers to figure out the craziness my friends and I witnessed daily was made for TV drama.

The dope was getting folks high as a kite. From ballplayers to politicians and other quote-unquote socialites, everybody was snorting the white. My eyes lit up when I tagged along with the older hustlers on a trip to downtown and South Beach. I couldn't believe people had the kind of money to buy the cars I saw. Porsches, Ferraris, and Lamborghinis were all on display. I used to peer out the window of the beat-up Lincoln I rode in. Of course I daydreamed. Those dudes were raking in cheese. A lot of cheese.

In those days the name Pablo Escobar was legendary. Imagine some kind of fairy-tale *Wizard of Oz* where all dreams came true. Well, Colombia was Oz and Escobar was the wizard. But of course to some poor black kids all that land could be was fantasy. Word around the campfire was that cats like Mundey were actually starting connecting with the wizard himself. When they brought the white girl back, they flew down the western coast of Florida. Every hustler back then did the same. Whether it was weed coming from the islands or blow from Colombia, narcs wouldn't think a plane heading south from Georgia was packed with powder. That route was off the drug-trafficking radar. Mundey and Roberts even built their own airport runway. They were some bold dudes who continued to get bolder.

Sometimes they had it dropped near the Bahamas, where boats would bring it in. I always daydreamed of finding a stray package floating along the bay, like those found by a couple of older cats in my neighborhood who worked on the docks cleaning the drug runners' speedboats. I knew some of those dudes had to steal a couple of bricks. At five I was game enough to do it, but I was too young to be working down by the docks. I would have tucked that brick in a garbage bag and run as far away as I could. I would have run all the way to Georgia, even South Carolina. Finding a stray package in the bay was like wishing upon a star. It was only wishful thinking of course. For now, I could only listen to the stories.

Powder was flooding Miami. Club owners were letting folks snort in their nightclubs. As if God was playing a joke on poor religious folks, one Sunday a shower of bricks even crashed through the roof of a church. About 80 percent of America's cocaine was coming from Miami. The news headlines showed that the country was in a recession. I remember folks got really strapped for cash at that time. Alongside the police brutality, the lack of cash flow sent folks over the edge during the riots, but judging from all the cars, jewelry, and mansions downtown, you would never have known it. Dope runners even doled out six figures on bulletproof cars.

Panama's dictator Manuel Noriega allowed dealers to launder their millions through the country's banks, but some of those dudes had too much cash. They buried the excess in their lawns or paid folks to stash it in their homes.

If they weren't at the horse races, they spent their cash at a ritzy spot called the Mutiny Hotel. But my city is like a pretty chick that's good-looking from afar but really far from good-looking when you get in bed with her. All that money was sure to lead to bloodletting. You can't dangle a ham hock in front a starved dog and not expect to get bitten. The party would be soon over, at least in *their* part of town.

14

Survivin' the Drought

THE RIDE SOUTH ON THE PALMETTO EXPRESSWAY, A
six-lane highway that takes you into the heart of suburban southwest Miami and farther into citrus country, offers one of the
most breathtaking sunsets in all South Florida. It's where you
go to escape the urban madness. Folks who had already stacked
some cheese bought a nice home in Pinecrest, the Falls, and
Cutler Ridge. South Beach was too risqué, so to speak, to raise
a family. Shit, with all that dope dealing and whoredom going
down near downtown, those neighborhoods offered a more se-
rene atmosphere.

White folks were hightailing it out of there as the Cubans,
Haitians, Trinidadians, and Jamaicans were moving in. The
whites either moved down south or north to Fort Lauderdale.

The current upscale hoods like Miramar and Pembroke Pines between Fort Lauderdale and Miami didn't really exist yet. The traffic as you went southwest was crazy, but like I said earlier, the ambience was off the chain. As Miami's skyline fades in the background, cloudless blue skies loom above and tomato fields glow under violet and orange hues in the foreground until Dadeland Mall interrupts the suburban bliss. So when some crazy Colombians lit the place afire on July 11, 1979, folks in Miami knew the U.S. government would soon step in.

If ever there was a stereotype about Latin folks, the one about them being passionate and hot-tempered has to stick. When they get to popping off, someone call the coroner. It's a catch-22. That Latin influence is part of what makes Miami hot and sizzling to the rather dull and mundane rest of America. Latin and Caribbean folks give our city character, but that Wednesday they scared the living daylight out of white folks.

Two cats armed with machine guns walked into a Crown Liquors and blasted a couple rivals, then sprayed the parking lot. They let off eighty rounds from the kinds of weapons that would have made Rambo look like Andy Griffith.

That year more than 400 were murdered in Miami. In 1980, 567 were murdered, followed by 621 the following year. The city had to bring in a moving morgue. Sadly enough, as young as I was, I wanted in on the action. Kids didn't play cowboys and Indians in the Beans. We used to pretend to be dope traffickers, even faking the foreign accents sometimes.

As if that wasn't enough, Fidel Castro did the unthinkable a couple months after the McDuffie riots. I have to give it to Castro. He is one bold and crafty old dude. He continuously gives America his ass to kiss with impunity. He opened Cuba's prisons. The Mariel Boatlift was a spectacle. How do I say this while trying to be politically correct? I can't. Castro sent over the *niggas*. That's what good American folk will try to shy away from saying, so I just said it for them. The media and Republicans had a field day of course. They blamed all of Miami's ills on some poor folks who just came over here for a better life. How did people from an impoverished Caribbean island come into assault rifles and MAC-10s?

The U.S. government has always blamed black folks for their mishaps. Those Cuban cats became what I call honorary niggas. Black folks should have given them and the other Caribbean cats a nigga handbook to follow that outlines the ins and outs of coping with day-to-day stresses such as driving while black.

If you get pulled over, dragged out your vehicle, and smacked across the head with a baton, your casualty minority insurance should cover it. Don't take it personal. It's part of the protocol that comes with being colored in America. Get used to it.

Blacks around my way were blind to the hypocrisy. They saw our new neighbors as competition for the scraps thrown out by the *man*. In my opinion the Cubans, Haitians, and other Caribbean folks helped us. They came over here and gave those crackers their ass to kiss. I got love for all my *chicos* and Haitians. They stuck together, which is something we African-Americans are still trying to learn how to do.

As far as I saw it, our worst enemy was and still is ourselves. The sad truth is niggas don't like niggas. Too many of us drink the Kool-Aid served by Democrats who give us the victim card while they watch us wallow in our own ignorance. I can't get mad at a Haitian or Cuban for coming over here and snatching the goody bag you were taking your sweet time to pick up. Look at American history. Those Pilgrims didn't ask Chief Running Wolf or whatever his name was if they could squat on his sacred patch of prairie. They put a gun to his head, then ran in the tepee and boned Pocahontas. Whatever opportunities blacks thought they were supposed to have, they should have taken. They didn't, so others did.

The racist media coverage caused by the Boatlift and the violence was ridiculous. Before *CSI: Miami*, there was *Miami Vice*. People soaked in the images of lawlessness. The movie *Scarface* solified the stereotype. Imagine seeing a movie showcase all the madness happening around you. We all related to Tony Montana, whether you were a black kid in the Beans, a Haitian praying for better days over at Notre Dame de Catholic, or a Cuban cabbie toughing it out in Little Havana. But the movie destroyed Miami's image. That was followed by some jackass at *Time* magazine who wrote a cover story declaring Miami a "paradise lost." The FBI started cracking down on all the kingpins. Runners like Willy Falcon and Sal Magluta who used the Opa-locka airport to make coke deliveries in the heart of the city came under the microscope. Those dudes made Mundey and Roberts look like Little Leaguers in the dope game. At their prime they made about $2 billion. From paying for ads to look for potential witnesses then having them killed, those two Miami Senior High School dropouts were accused of doing it all. A former *Miami Herald* reporter, Jack DeVoe, was their courier. The dude got sick of reporting the news and became it. Even scenes from *Miami Vice* were a bit too *authentic*. Several episodes of *Miami Vice* were filmed at the mansion owned by Willy Martinez, a well-known kingpin. Miami's cocaine allure was addictive.

The powers that be promised to double the police force, but they had to lower their induction standards to find the manpower. That was the dumbest thing they ever did. I've never given the boys in blue any rave reviews, but that decision had to put the Miami-Dade police department in the *Guinness World Book of Idiots*. When a good cop turns bad, he's gone forever.

Unhappy with the low salary, many of the new, mostly Cuban recruits waged an all-out war on dealers. Those cops formed a rip-off crew that executed smugglers. They were actually holding dealers hostage. I would have paid to see the look on those dudes' faces when Officer Suarez was taking their dope.

You have the right to turn over the bricks, sucker.

They stole more than seven hundred kilos of powder that came in on the boats up the Miami River. One cop, Alex Marrero, went to prison for offering protection to one of the smugglers for $300,000. Remember him? He was the same cop acquitted of killing Arthur McDuffie back in 1980. The Miami River Cops, as they were called, made cocaine accessible to locals outside ritzy Miami Beach and Brickell Avenue. Prices on the white girl dropped. She went to the highest bidder. You could say Miami's cocaine economy was democratized. Those cops made it snow on my side of the bridge.

That part of Miami's cocaine history the filmmakers and media didn't get to. They never showed who chopped it up and broke it down. You never saw who got addicted and whose lives were destroyed. The joke always seems to be played on black folks. They got rich and we did the time. They cheated us. Unlike those white cats whose motivation was greed and power, we were just trying to survive. Criminals aren't born; they're created. We got that messed up hand with no aces or dueces and played it the best we could.

Cocaine wasn't even meant for poor folk. It wasn't for us. The only people who could afford to use it back then were professionals. Doctors, lawyers, teachers, and cops were all getting high off it. When it came to the hood, blacks started smoking it. They started inhaling the vapors from cocaine. Freebasing is what we called it. It offered a more potent high than snorting. It even lasted longer.

On Friday nights my mother, uncles, and aunts would go in the bedroom and lock the door. They thought we didn't know what they were doing, but we did. They were in there getting high as a kite. I was too young to have an opinion, but I didn't like the way Pearl's mood changed when she was high on the white.

The lasting effect of freebasing was worse than from snorting. That's why people in powerful positions are doing coke weekly. Don't think the pillars of our community aren't getting high on the white right now. They're what people may call functional coke users. I sold it to my fair share of doctors and lawyers when I was out there hustling. I was lucky because the average dope boy couldn't get it to those folks, so dealers got economical. They cooked the freebased form of cocaine with baking soda to stretch it.

Enter crack rock or what we called boulders.

That's right. The birth of a drug that caused so much pain in society and wiped out the black inner city was purely economical. Black folks have always been good at getting the most for their buck. We're some of the world's best bargain shoppers. Take a stroll down Harlem's 125th Street or Queens' Jamaica Avenue if you don't believe me.

Folks wanted to get high faster and longer for cheaper. The profits from a dime rock—$10 worth of crack—didn't compare to what someone could make from $10 worth of cocaine, a dime soft. However, most couldn't even afford that. Those smokers were so hard up for cash, we ended up selling a nickel rock and sometimes $2 and $3 hits. I got lucky when I came across a juggler once a week who could afford a dime rock. A juggler was a dope boy's favorite smoker. Those with a lot of money could get a lot of hits. Someone with less would get a smaller hit, but there was something to be sold. That's really how crack became more popular than cocaine.

We didn't stop there of course.

We got creative with the white girl. Imagine going to a house party in the hood where Kool-Aid often tastes like it has a million different flavors. It's because the party's host ran out of one flavor. Folks start adding other mixes to make it happen. It was no different with the drugs. We added cocaine to the weed joint and called it boonk or dirty. We even added the powder to cigarettes and called it a chopper. Of course all this mixing and stretching made the dope more lethal.

The dope game was the black man's only way out as far as I saw it. I know that sounds like a cliché, but don't judge me until you stand in those shoes. In Miami the option was to be a pimp or dope boy. If someone was born in the hood in Miami around 1975, his or her mother had dated or was messing with a pimp or dope boy. Somebody in their family was doing something illegal.

Any brother in the hood who was a street-level dealer never thought he could have gotten rich. By the time it reached our hood, too many people had dabbled in it and made their cut already. When folks ask how could I sell poison to my own people, I say that's an unfair question. The world isn't that black-and-white. It isn't that cut-and-dry. I respond with introspection. What if I don't value myself or my community? Dealers are as much addicts as the users. We both have the virus, but one is just succumbing to the disease faster. We live in a messed-up society. Besides, it would have got to my people if we didn't get it to them. We weren't the problem, but we most definitely didn't help the problem.

In the hood they called us the Get High Boys.

After the McDuffie riots, no jobs or opportunities came to black Miami. I, Dante, Bodeem, HB, Tater, and Tronne were just some ghetto kids looking for an economic savior. We tried to find it in cocaine. Hollywood showed us how.

15

Pimp

BEFORE THE DOPE BOY COULD TAKE OVER THE block, he had to contend with the pimps. They were the original hood superstars. Prostitution was the main means of getting money before coke dealing. People usually point toward Chicago and Detroit when they talk about pimping. I'm sure those cities had their share of Archbishop Don Juans, but Miami brought swagger to the hustle. Let's face it. Where else can a woman strut around half-naked with her goodies exposed for most of the year? Bob Marley had to be high on the good green thinking about Miami when he wrote "Pimper's Paradise."

Like most hustles, pimping came down to who had the slickest tongue. A guy had to talk a woman out of her right reasoning to get her to walk down a strip selling her love below. There was an art to it. The prevalence of pimping can make someone speculate on those ironies rampant in the hood.

Imagine if those pimps could have got into city hall? I always thought pimps would have made good politicians. There isn't much difference to the two professions. Both are selling you bullshit to get something out of you.

Paul Red and the Bel-Air Blondes made it look easy.

They were what folks could call signature pimps in the hood. Of course there were more too numerous to mention, but the way those two put it down was smooth like Hennessy chased with caramel drops.

Red always wore the brightest zoot suits. He showcased the hot pink, lime green, and of course the obvious red. His game was what people called mack-certified.

"Damn, damn, damn, damn!" Red would yell, walking up to a lady in a bar. "Looky here, woman, you got me intoxicated and I ain't had a drink yet. I'm sure you fit that glass slipper!"

The lady would smile.

"Bartender! Please get Cinderella the house special. I got to whisk her away before Prince Charming comes looking for her!" boasted Red.

In minutes the two were locked in conversation. Red had the magic words. Some cats just had that golden tongue. You can't teach someone how to mack. It has to be in his DNA.

Months later the same lady would be out on the strip in broad daylight shuffling down Seventeenth Avenue, all broken-down and destitute, another of Red's whores. Money is a powerful motivator.

Women turned tricks in the alley behind my apartment.

They turned tricks under the bleachers by the basketball court. Any discreet corner or shaded space became a john's rented spot.

The Bel-Air Blondes were a crew of older pimps. They were always decked out in white. They wore their hair in processed curls and donned brightly colored shirts with butterfly collars and bell-bottom pants to accentuate their white suits. Their square-toe gator shoes were classic. They drove Lincoln town cars. Long, black, shiny Lincolns were their pimp caravan. With Curtis Mayfield crooning from their stereos they cruised the block checking on their ladies.

"Looking good, Ms. America. You know daddy likes his on the first of the month, baby!"

"Trust me, I got your rent, daddy!"

The pimps treated their trade with class. There was order and a code of conduct to the game. No pimp disrespected another pimp's strip. Any disagreements were settled over a shot of cognac.

Most folks frowned upon the pimps and their whores. Tell me what's different when a woman goes on a date with a man who expects to get sex after he pays for dinner? Women fly into South Beach from all over America, hoping to meet some rich guy in a nightclub. They dream of moving out of their boring desk job and into a mansion on the beach. Then they scheme on how to get knocked up to win the child-support lottery. That defines tricking if you ask me.

That was the more subtle way women tricked back in those days. Our women in Miami are what you might call traditional females. They are accustomed to being taking care of, if you know what I mean. Save that feminist, Ms. Independent crap for up North. In Miami, a man has to wine and dine a lady. Women got all dolled up on the weekend in hopes of finding themselves a man with money.

In fact, that's how Miami ended up having so many strip clubs. Most of our strip clubs were regular clubs until women decided they would just take their tricking on the weekends further. Men went to happy hour to find what we call a shone today. A shone is a lady that a guy just wants to hang out and kick it with. Women wanted to find a man who could spend the most money. The pimps shined in that respect.

I looked up to them. Every boy in the hood did. Our admiration stemmed from basic economics. Whoever in the projects was self-sufficient without food stamps gained notoriety. The pimps were some cold, debonair cats, and theirs was a nonviolent trade, so to speak. They were from the old school of hustling and knew violence was bad for business. Drama isn't good for concealing illegal activity. That's why it's so easy to weed out authentic gangsters from the fake ones. No true gangster wants to attract attention. It's not the way the game is played. When gunshots rang out, the boys in blue sped down the avenue.

Most cops who patrol the hood know the drug dealers and hustlers. It's a necessary and uneasy friendship. The cops let those crooks conduct business year-round. They only get involved when an innocent kid or a bystander gets shot in the cross fire. Do you really think the Miami-Dade police department launches an investigation when a known drug dealer gets put to sleep?

Hell no!

Good riddance. Let those niggers kill themselves.

The pimps understood that there could be some form of honor among thieves. They kept their whores happy on the finest drugs and gave each other the mutual respect earned over years of illegal living. However, when the powder came, the pimps lost their footing. Cadillac cars replaced Lincolns, and the hustlers behind the wheels were a more sinister and flashy breed.

I can still remember that Saturday night at Green's Lounge when folks noticed the game was changing. Everyone realized that dope would soon bring out the worst in all of us.

Green's Lounge was a typical down-South pub where black folk went to unwind. Booze, gossip, and good laughs were a mainstay. Ribs blazing on the grill and catfish frying sent a soul food aroma floating throughout the place. Lots of brawls always occurred at the lounge. The fisticuffs often interrupted the usual weekend bliss where old men sat playing dominoes and couples swayed to Marvin Gaye near the jukebox.

Amid that cool atmosphere cats would also get all fired up on devil's water, aka moonshine, and start breaking stuff. Shortly after the fighting ensued, the bartender would calm the two winos down, and the good times continued. It was a place scripted in the usual down-South country drama.

I was an avid pool player. Even to this day I can rack 'em and knock 'em down better than the average pool shark. It's one the few pastimes that I can truthfully say helped me escape mentally. On that particular night, I was beating the hog skin off the behind of some older cats.

"That boy right there the truth! I told y'all buddy got a mean pool game!" Smitty the bartender yelled.

"I'm taking all bets that he'll whup you proper!"

I was kicking that old-timer's ass.

Meanwhile, an old pimp was trying to get the attention of a guy at the bar. The guy whose attention he sought looked to be no older than twenty. He was flirting with a chick at the bar. She was obviously one of the pimp's women.

"Hey, partner, you're tying up little Ms. Lady's ears with all the sweet talk. Good conversation don't come cheap these days," the old dude said.

The two kept on talking. The young guy shrugged his shoulders. For any older hustler in the pimp game the gesture was just as disrespectful as a smack in the face. The pimp didn't take kindly to the insult.

"Partner, I ain't gonna tell you again to ease up off the lady if there isn't going to be a monetary exchange," the pimp said.

"We're just conversating! Why you got to be all in my business all the time!" the woman snapped back.

"Ho, your business is my business!" the pimp fired back, and slapped her.

The sound echoed throughout the bar. That lady got smacked hard. I thought her head would have tumbled off. The young guy stood up. He reached in his pocket, then threw a stack of hundreds in the pimp's face. I wanted to run and grab the money that fell, but knew better.

"Motherfucker!" The pimp sprang on him.

Then all I saw was blood shooting upward to the ceiling. The young hustler kept jamming a knife in the pimp's neck.

Folks tried to pry him off the old dude, but it was too late. I never saw so much blood in my life. It was the first time I saw a man killed.

Something was happening in Miami. The pimps were losing their footing. Hoe strolls were soon becoming dope holes. The prostitutes turned into addicts. Pimps became hollow shells of their former selves. Those durable enough sailed the tide and made the transition to selling powder. Others succumbed to it.

16

Gangsta Libin'

It began with Mr. Biggs. He was the original Miami gangster, in every sense of the word. Biggs wore khaki Dickies pants and a T-shirt. His legacy will be left in the hands of Miami historians to debate over. Law enforcement will view him as common dope-dealing hustler, an inner-city scourge who preyed on misguided young men in search of a father figure. He stood well over six feet tall with a laugh just as imposing. They will call the hood's adoration for him a case of misplaced priorities. But in my hood we didn't see doctors, lawyers, and teachers whom we could aspire to become.

In our imperfect world Biggs made do with what he was given. In ghetto politics the means most definitely justifies the ends. In the end he showed young guys and the community alike what a black man could turn from the hustle. In the absence of real economic opportunities, Biggs was a one-man enterprise. He started with a quaint gardening company and soon started building homes. He bought up real estate and employed young dudes who would otherwise find themselves stealing from working folks. The powder was good to Biggs and he was good to us.

When the local theater was in danger of shutting down, he bought the place and turned it into Heart of the City. It was one of the few times Biggs put his wealth on display. His foot-long, gold Rolls-Royce pendant looked like it weighed a ton.

Heart of the City was the most happening nightclub in the city back then. All the hustlers and ladies who flocked behind them came out. It was a lavish affair. For those couple of hours on Friday and Saturday night folks in the Beans escaped the urban grind, losing themselves in the music and booze. There in that tight space while bumping and grinding to the Funkadelics, folks found temporary respite.

A true dope man gives back to his community, and that's exactly what Biggs did. When he went to prison, a lot of folks lost jobs and their livelihood.

His younger contemporary Prince Rick was also an old-school gangster, but with more flare. The home Rick built on two lots in Carol City was never before seen in the hood. That *Scarface*-style mansion was smooth. Inside, Rick had one of his Rolls-Royces on display. In Opa-locka, Freddy Ice, who folks called the real mayor, had opened a gym so the young dudes could take their frustrations out on punching bags. It was the closest thing to a Boys and Girls Club near the Triangle. It wasn't unusual to spot a line of kids running up to Ice as he passed out wads of cash. The dealers were our Santa Claus.

Then of course there was Drop Top Mo. Mo turned wherever he went into a movie set. Everyone on the strip was his costar. He made us all dreamers. He cut the tops off all his cars and hung out in Las Vegas with Mike Tyson. Any hustler that could sip champagne with Iron Mike was a superstar in my eyes. Tyson, the most feared brother on the planet, was that guy every true hustler wanted to break bread with. Hustlers from up North came down to see how Miami's hustlers lived. It's who they were getting their dope from anyhow.

My father, Charles "Pop" Young, was also heavy in the streets back then. Pimping. Dope slinging. Gambling. You name it and Pop did it. Like Biggs, he was one of those original Miami gangsters, and sadly those hustling ways left him no room for the raising and nurturing of kids. Pop has too many sons to count. I think fate played some joke and birthed a whole flock of us who, up until this point in my life story, seemed genetically disposed to dope dealing as well. Only two of my brothers, Chuck and Ephraim, share the same mother.

My brother Derrick "Hollywood" Harris was Pop's favorite son. He was the shining star among the younger breed of dope boys on the rise when those gangsters previously mentioned bowed out the game. If someone could paint a perfect picture of a tragic hero, it would be Hollywood.

The ladies loved his good looks. The hood loved his

generosity, and the killers feared his gangster heart. I told more people Hollywood was my brother than I've told Pop was my father. Ironically, the anger we both shared for Pop is what drew us close. I don't think any younger brother admired and loved his older brother more than I did Wood. He was only two years my senior, but in my eyes he might as well have been a superhero. He was truly one of Miami's thug angels.

17

Living in a World

"ALWAYS KEEP IT ONE HUNDRED."

That phrase was Wood's favorite. It defined his character. Whatever decision one makes in this life, make sure one believes in it to the fullest. Go hard or don't go at all. People stand behind those who are sincere in their actions. No one respects someone who lives life sideways. Wood preached those phrases daily. If he turned his pistol on a man and that man shot him first, Wood wished the shooter the best in his future life—even if the bullet landed Wood in a wheelchair. Wood believed people have to live with the consequences of each decision. One must take the good and the bad.

When I first moved down to south Miami-Dade, I had to gain a foothold. The resident tough guys in the hoods south of downtown Miami in neighborhoods like Ghouls, Perrine, Naranja, and Richmond Heights weren't going to let me come down there and disrespect them. Cutler Manor, Chocolate City, and Rainbow City all looked a lot like the Beans. There were crap games, hookers, and dope houses. It's never personal when one steps onto another man's turf and he takes the offensive. It's just the way of the hood. In a puppy litter the weak puppy most likely dies. Dudes prey on soft cats in the projects.

The fighting wasn't personal. We knocked each other out, then dusted each other off and commenced breaking bread. My reputation had already hit down south. Hollywood had told everybody about his "wild" younger brother raising hell in the Beans.

The look on Wood's face when I got down there was classic. He looked me up and down and shook his head. I'd been wearing the same stained T-shirt, torn jeans, and cruddy sneakers for two days. I even smelled bad.

"My little brother got to stay fresh always," he said.

Wood was generous. If someone came around him, he took care of them. If Wood ate filet mignon, his friends ate filet mignon. Wood went to his closet and threw me a pair of black Dickies shorts and a pair of brand-new Travel Foxes. Those shoes were the status symbol back then. Wood rocked the British Knights sneakers and matching jumpsuit. No one in the hood was fresh as that. He even had a block phone. His jewelry was blinding. People called my brother Hollywood for a reason.

"Try those on," said Wood. "Yeah, now buddy looking right."

He pulled a wad of cash from his pocket. It looked like a stack of thousands. Up until then I thought that kind of cash was reserved for the older dope boys. I was dead wrong. Wood was getting money like he had been in the game for over a decade. He handed me a couple hundred dollars.

"This is yours right here," he said.

Outside, the parking lot mirrored a car show. Wood had about a dozen cars. He had pairs of Mercedes-Benzes, BMWs, and Maximas. The older hustlers liked driving Chevys and Lincolns. Wood had those, but he also had a fondness for the foreign cars.

I couldn't believe my eyes. First and foremost I was proud. I knew my father was making a lot of money as well, but we didn't have much of a relationship so I didn't care. Hollywood showed me love. He took me under his wings.

That weekend he took me to Ghoul's Park. It's where everyone hung out. Dudes were playing basketball and others were freestyling rap lyrics. The park was where folks flossed back in those days. I didn't really have much leisure time when I stayed in the Beans, and I think Hollywood knew this. So he made sure to take me everywhere he went. He introduced me to Dante, Tronne, Tater, Bodeem, and HB.

"This that wild nigga I was telling y'all about," he told them.

I didn't say anything at first. I wasn't shy. I was just sizing those dudes up. It's not a cliché when cats in the street say real recognizes real. One can usually look a person in the eyes and get a glimpse of what's in his soul. Someone who's hiding something will rarely or hardly ever look you in the eyes. Dante stared into mine.

"What's up homey? Wood said you a problem up in the city!" he chuckled.

"Nah, bruh. I just don't take kindly to dudes trying me," I answered.

They all laughed.

"Told y'all the nigga is a problem," said Wood.

Before long we were all connected at the hip. Hollywood was on the road a lot, bringing the white girl into Miami. He was making money in Georgia, Virginia, and the Carolinas. I think Wood was even making money as far as Chicago. Back then, any weight coming through Miami was being picked up. The port was just too hot. So Wood had his supplier do what Mundey and Roberts did. He had it flown to Georgia and driven down.

I was itching to get my hands on the powder. All that money I saw made me daydream, but I had just got thrown out the Beans and caused Pearl so much hell that I tried my hand at school one last time. Besides, high school was right around the corner. That's when the honeys really start to look good. The main motivation for me and the other fourteen-year-old boys entering the ninth grade were the ladies. That's when girls started looking voluptuous. I couldn't wait.

18

Strong Woman

AT DIFFERENT INTERVALS IN ONE'S LIFE GOD ALWAYS sends someone to take a meaningful interest in you. I don't care who you are. From the pillars of society to the inmates serving life sentences, God will send you an angel. If someone's too stupid to take the angel's advice, that's their problem. When I was a little kid, He sent Booner and Junior. I didn't listen so I got myself thrown out the Beans. This time He sent my stepmother, Lynn.

My father was home for only a couple of weeks before he was sent back to prison. He was living the hustler's life, as people call it. It was one of the more than ten times he made it back to prison. So Lynn was stuck with me and my yet unborn brother, Non Stop. She didn't run from the responsibility.

Like Pearl, Lynn had that type of die-hard resiliency that black women embody. I believe God knew the hardships faced by black men would leave their women out in the cold. So he made them strong. The strength black women possess can't be found elsewhere. Throughout history they've had to defend households while their men were carted off to slavery and later the industrial factories. In my hood the dope game was to blame for the absenteeism.

Lynn was a Seventh-Day Adventist. She spent weekends in church. When she wasn't there, she worked the graveyard shift. We alternated days to take care of the household. I took some days off at school. She took some days off at work. Lynn tried to provide the best home possible for me where Pearl left off.

Meanwhile, in the classroom Mr. Fudge worked hard to get me back into high school. The school board had actually given me another shot. I won't ever say something too damaging about the Miami-Dade public school system. They really tried with Maurice Young. After I left Jan Mann, I was sent to another alternative program, called JR Lee, but sure enough I was kicked out of there, too. Project Lee was the last stop on the dropout train. It was where they sent your sorry ass when no other school wanted you. I thought the place would be a mini-vacation before I got permanently thrown out of public high schools. The streets were waiting. I was looking forward to hustling a full twenty-four-hour day. I went to my first class and did what was expected of me. I went to sleep.

"Boy, get your ass up! This look like the damn Holiday Inn to you?" The hand at my shirt collar woke me indeed. Mr. Fudge was bearing down on me like a pit bull at his last meal. I clutched my pen. "I wish you would try and stab me! I'll knock your ass out!" Fudge yelled. "Walking round here looking like the sorry nigga folks think you are."

Everyone in the class sat upright. I thought Fudge was out of his mind. The guy had to have a screw or two loose. Didn't he know the last teacher brave enough to use me as his manhood sounding board ended up with a concussion and put on bed rest for two weeks?

He answered my thoughts. "Trust me, I ain't Tuttle's punk ass! I'll get me evil on you, boy. If you wanna fuck your life up, do it on your own time!" he fumed.

I straightened up, then contemplated fighting. But something about Fudge intrigued me. The dude came to class wearing Dickies shorts and a Malcolm X T-shirt. His shoes were cream-colored wallabies. He reminded me of a hustler in the street. He also had heart.

Fudge was no more than five feet one inch, if he was even five feet. In that class, filled to capacity with misfits, he was taking a big risk by threatening a student. Gangs of students jumped teachers routinely. A good number of teachers spent time in the hospital. Teachers in those alternative programs were actually risking their lives, showing up for an ungodly $30,000 annual salary. But that's another story. I could spend hours discussing the exploitation of the folks we entrust to educate our kids.

When Fudge noticed he'd got my attention, he fixed my collar. He walked back to the chalkboard, grabbed a piece of chalk, and wrote in cap-size letters: S-T-U-P-I-D. Students squirmed in their seats.

"That's how you look to folks. You look like a bunch of dummies," said Fudge. "You walk around laughing while you throw your lives away. Are you stupid, young blood?" Fudge pointed the chalk my way.

"Nah," I replied.

I aced most math quizzes when I gave even a 10 percent effort. English and grammar were my favorite subjects. With all the bullshit going on in my hood, I enjoyed writing short stories. Those fictional characters I made up took me far away from the Beans. In minutes, Fudge got all of us teenage misfits to sit transfixed, hanging on every word he uttered.

His story mirrored most of ours. He told us about growing up in the projects. We could relate to Fudge. Folks think ghetto children always need some ballplayer or movie star to pop up in the hood for kids to listen. Kids see right through that. They may be excited for the first ten minutes, but they know that celebrity is going back to his fantasy life far away from where they are. It doesn't take a million bucks in your bank account to be a hero. All one has to do is take an interest. Fudge gave a damn.

Most of the kids in Project Lee just wanted someone to piss their way. They wanted someone to take notice for five seconds. That's why you have to pay attention to kids when they begin to misbehave. They spend years kicking and screaming for attention. When that doesn't work, they shoot and rob. By that time the courts say lock their sorry asses up. They can get all the attention they need staring eye to eye with a crazed cellmate. Fudge told us about our roots in Africa.

"That's right. We were kings and queens before they hauled us over here in chains," Fudge would say. "Young blood, you got royal blood flowing through your veins." Fudge said I was related to kings and queens. For a kid growing up in the Beans amid the addicts, hookers, and winos, this knowledge was earth-shattering. That some young dude my age who looked like me back in Ghana was being called prince rocked my world. He probably had some hot girl powdering his pecker.

Up until that point, we only learned that we were slaves. Black history began and ended with my ancestor calling some white guy massa. Fudge's lessons gave me confidence. I really looked up to Fudge. He made me believe I could become something worthwhile. I completed my eighth-grade requirements and earned my seat in the ninth grade. I was there only several weeks before the inevitable happened. I just wasn't cut out for the classroom.

19

Going Down Like That

GHOUL'S PARK WAS DEFINITELY THE PLACE TO CHILL with the crew on the weekends. Unfortunately, rivalries were born there as well. The weekend before school started, I was hanging with the crew. By now, Dante, Tronne, Tater, Bodeem, and I were a bona fide band of brothers. The morning ritual began with a dollar's worth of chicken wings at the corner store. Whoever had the cash picked up the tab. Nigel and Onk joined us in the park that Saturday. They were always close by, but were more focused on sports than trouble. If they had a problem with guys from the streets, we handled it for them. That Saturday an argument ensued about a topic of gargantuan importance:

"Bruh, I'm telling you, Kim got the fattest ass this side of

Perrine. I wanna get me a little piece of that right there," said Dante.

"Nah, bruh, Kiesha definitely got her beat," Tronne chimed in.

We all nodded in agreement. Then Big Black and Shrimp came walking toward us. Black was a guy one may call the resident hood star. He was a year younger than me, but got respect from Hollywood and the other hustlers down south. Black was one of those cats whose heart was that of a man twice his size. He took a liking to me and it was much appreciated. Anybody Black cosigned was a force to be reckoned with. The ground shook when Black walked. Some people have a presence that commands respect. Black was that type of person. He wasn't having it. His right-hand man, Shrimp, was just as respected.

"Everything good?" asked Black.

"Yeah, Dante over here saying Kim got a fatter ass than Kiesha," said Tronne.

"Why y'all don't ask Maurice? He hit both of 'em," Black said, turning toward me.

I shook my head. It was no secret that I was popular with the girls. I was Hollywood's younger brother. He had girls from Homestead to Fort Lauderdale and every town in between. They had sisters. They liked my eclectic persona.

I know it sounds suspect that I would describe myself in such a colorful fashion, but I always stood out. I added my own style to the fresh gear Wood laced me with. I wore a dashiki shirt with my black Dickies pants and topped it all off with a gleaming gold-nugget bracelet. Chicks dug my style. Women always go for the guys that are confident enough to stand on their own. Don't follow the crowd if you want the ladies. You don't have to take my word for it. Go do your research. Some of my girls I was really serious about even if I couldn't admit it to the crew.

But in the hood a guy wasn't given the option of sharing his girlfriend. It was a requirement. My friend had the right to my girl in much the same way he had a right to my chicken wings. That I actually had, and have always had, the utmost respect for women was a secret I kept from the crew. I couldn't have them thinking I was soft. I treated the ladies with class. That was my secret. A ten-step handbook to pimping doesn't exist. I was charming. I despised the way older men took advantage of younger women. They filled their impressionable minds with all sorts of dreams, then left them out in the cold nine months pregnant without a pot to piss in. It still ticks me off to this day when I see a teenage girl on the bus stop stuck with a baby carriage, bearing the weight of the world on her shoulders. If I could send a heat-seeking missile toward every deadbeat father on the planet, I would. Put everything I love on that. Women like sweetness, and I was all the above. Of course I kept it gangster with my crew. So they had liberties to all my girls. Well, all of my girls except Tiffany. I had a fondness for her. She was about five feet five inches with a caramel complexion and the brightest brown eyes this side of the Mississippi. Honestly, I was crazy about her. So I tried hard to keep her far away from Lou and Ty.

Lou and Ty took the concept of "it ain't no fun if the homeys can't have none" too far. Some older cats just didn't take no for an answer. I should have known better when I decided to get some sugar over there. My stepmother didn't take kindly to having all of my "little fast hussies" as she called them running through the house. I'd been wining and dining Tiffany for months, acting like her real-life Casanova, shelling out money like I was an ATM. It was Wood's money. He thought I was spending it at the arcade. When she finally decided to give me the goodies, I couldn't wait. I needed a place to do the do. Lou and Ty told me I could get busy by their pad for $50. It was pretty steep, but I was hard-pressed to see what Tiffany had up under that skirt.

When we showed up, those two were in the living room bagging crack rocks and counting money. Perfect. It seemed to be the only time Lou and Ty wouldn't talk your head off. Tiffany was scared, shaking like drugstore jelly.

"You sure we're okay in here?" she whispered, tugging on my shirt.

I couldn't hear anything. I was too busy imagining the positions I saw in that *Kama Sutra* book I'd found in Wood's bedroom. When those chicks left Wood's bedroom, they looked like they had seen the pearly gates, so I studied that book through and through.

"I don't like the way they're looking at me," she repeated.

"Girl, those fools ain't paying attention to you," I said.

They were.

I led her up the bedroom stairs. All those earrings, movies, and sneakers she enjoyed were about to pay off. I started kissing on her neck, then delved down toward Eden. I reached in my back pocket. It wasn't there. I nearly tore through my pocket.

You have to be kidding me. My rubbers weren't there.

I was determined though.

"No, I don't wanna get pregnant," Tiffany fumed.

"We can do the old-fashioned birth control," I coaxed.

"Hell no, that's what my cousin Kima used and she got three kids!"

I raced down the stairs like a runaway slave and asked Lou and Ty if they had any. Of course they didn't. What girl in her right mind would let those greasy two huff and puff on top of her? I bolted up the block toward the corner store. The line was long as heck. I waited and waited. A million thoughts ran through my head. What if Tiffany had second thoughts? The old man in line in front of me was getting his Powerball tickets scratched off. That always puzzled me. In every corner store in the hood, someone is always playing the lotto. I bet rich folks don't play the lotto that much. Imagine if those folks saved the money they spent playing lotto. Right now this dude's lucky-number dreams were making my muff-diving a fading reality. A good fifteen minutes had passed when I finally banked the corner and reached the entrance to the house.

Tiffany was limping down the stairs shaking. I ran toward her.

She started wailing on me. "They wouldn't stop! They wouldn't stop!" she cried.

I tried to hug her but she punched me in the face. I ran inside. Ty was sitting on the couch with his shirt off. Lou was in the bathroom whistling. If I could have killed those two that day, I would have, but I knew better.

"What you all bent outta shape for? Fuck that ho, bruh," said Lou.

"That cherry sure was sweet though!" added Ty.

Taking a teenage girl's honor was a joke to them. They were shucking and jiving like they had just ate a slice a pizza. Shit like that happened all the time. Girls in the hood fall victim to a world that doesn't value them. If black boys in the ghetto aren't worth shit on society's scale, where do you think that leaves the girls? If you think the hood is scary to a boy, imagine a young girl growing up fatherless. Imagine trekking those narrow alleys, dodging and sidestepping advances from determined pimps and dazed addicts. Picture the tugs on your skirt, pinches and touches in private places. Rape is rampant in the hood. The harsh truth is the victims aren't really a priority so the police don't investigate.

That day on the bus Tiffany didn't speak. She sat numb. Her sobs faded into cold contempt as she stared off into space. I wanted to ask her if there was anything I could do, but I knew there wasn't. I took her there. It was my fault. We were just two young kids caught in a teenage moment, but in our environment simple joys could become lifelong nightmares in the blink of an eye.

We never spoke again. I tried calling, but her sister would answer. Eventually I got the point. Try explaining to someone's family that their daughter got raped because you left her alone with crazed drug dealers. You can't. I chalked it up for what it was. I kept that day a secret from my crew. I didn't want dudes humiliating Tiffany more than she had already been.

20

Represent

AFTER BLACK SPILLED THE BEANS, THE CREW STARTED their interrogation.

"Damn, bruh! What it shake like? Kim look like she got hydraulics on that booty!" joked Dante. "How you got that ho to give it up?"

"A true pimp doesn't give out the tools to his trade," I joked. "One day I'll give a handbook on pimp economics."

We all laughed. Black and Shrimp gave daps and headed toward the avenue. Those two were always on the move. I kind of knew they were destined to end up in some deep trouble. They had that aura around them that scared the living daylight out of folks.

Then I heard someone yell my name. Well, they didn't

exactly yell my name. It sounded more like "Hey, fuck nigga! Yeah, you with the dashiki on!"

It was about that time.

I mentioned earlier that when someone moves to another hood, some resident thugs always think they should try the new kid on the block. I had a rep already. Furthermore, I came from the Beans. The projects down south were no different from those in the city and just as deadly. But, truth be told, the Beans were more well-known, so a brawl with any kid moving to Ghouls was a sounding board for any local hood star on the come-up. I had seen these dudes before. I didn't pay them any mind the first time they gave me an unfriendly glance. They were trying to check my temperature so to speak.

In the hood softness is weakness. If someone scares easily, that someone is as good as dead. If I backed down to a challenge, this crew would kick my ass for the rest of eternity and so would everyone else. Real recognizes real. A gangster won't go through the trouble of testing another gangster because he knows the hell that's soon to follow. So folks prey on the weak. It could be something as simple as a guy asking to borrow money. Every time I said yes, that lets him know just how much sugar I have running through my veins. Soon I would end up paying his child support and getting extorted. Those cats in Ghouls saw my lack of response as an opening. They didn't know I was trying to save them from me. Back then, the thoughts I had running through my mind were downright scary. I didn't want to just fight you. I wanted to maim you. I was suffering on the inside. It carried over in my rage.

I was sent down here to escape that madness. These dudes weren't going to let me escape. Dante clenched his fist. Tronne and Tater did the same. Just five minutes ago we were deep in conversation about the finer curves of life. Now we were staring down a pack of wolves ready to break loose.

I struck first, smashing a Heineken bottle on the guy's head. Blood splattered everywhere. I shoved him to the ground and pounded his head into the dirt. I choked him. The more I hit him, the more I felt better. His crew scattered like they saw the devil. I figured as much from our first encounter. They looked like their hearts pumped Kool-Aid. They followed this loud-mouth for confidence.

I loved beating bullies I knew couldn't fight. I ran up close and punched them, taking away their first line of defense. It cut past all the loud talk and gibber-jabber. It's the same fighting technique Kimbo uses. He was a head buster when we were growing up, so it's not surprising that he's now demolishing opponents on a worldwide level.

By now, I was really getting the best of the loudmouth. Dante grabbed the back of my shirt and pulled me off the guy, now spitting up his own blood.

"Bruh, you're about to kill him," warned Dante. "The shit ain't that deep."

"That's what I want to do. I wanna kill him!"

My crew had to help Dante pry me off. When they did, I shrugged my shoulders and pushed Dante. I turned my back and headed toward the avenue. At that moment my crew realized that I was down for pretty much whatever those harsh streets would throw at us. Tears swelled in my eyes as I stormed up the block kicking bottles and soda cans.

I wiped my tears as soon as I saw Black running up toward me, his pistol in hand.

"Bruh, you good? Somebody messing with you? I'll handle it right now." Black would.

"Nah, bruh, just been arguing with my stepsister."

"Damn, she still giving you drama, hunh? You know that girl is her mama daughter. Well, you know I always got your back."

Black was always looking out for me. I'm sure Hollywood played a part, but Wood was the type to let me fight my own battles. He knew that at times he wouldn't be there to chase away the demons. Black respected Wood, but Black was just a good dude. He fit into the category of folks who kept it "one hundred." Instead of preying on the weak, Black protected the kid he felt had a good heart but a weak punch.

He did raise a serious concern though. My stepsister and I weren't getting along. Our issues stemmed from exactly why women shouldn't have kids from different men. Do what the Bible says. Get married and raise your kids with one mother and one father. If people followed what the good Lord commands, our lives would be a whole lot easier.

Soon enough I found myself spending less time at home after getting into a huge fight with my stepsister. We fought daily. Being an outsider was becoming second nature to me. By now I had already spent most of my early life drifting with nowhere to go.

I slept at Dante's house some nights to make it easier on Lynn. He lived right next door with his grandmother. So I hung out all day, then Dante snuck me in when his grandmother went to bed.

All those factors just increased my anger. I was spiraling out of control, but my behavior earned street credibility. People started fearing me. I wasn't the hardest because my punch was like Mayweather's but because I had the biggest heart. That in itself is misleading. I cared less for my own well-being than anybody else did for his in my neighborhood. I felt I had nothing to lose. Fighting a person who doesn't care about his own preservation is suicide. You won't win. Fear is the only thing that keeps people in check. Some among us are truly goodwilled, but the majority would do most anything if they could get away with it.

Back then, I couldn't think of someone who'd miss me if I died so I didn't give a damn. I was headed off a cliff with my eyes wide-open. Death would be a bonus. It would have taken me away from all this bullshit.

Still, Fudge's lessons followed me to that first day of school. I wanted to see if I could be that "prince" he always called me and the other boys at Project Lee. Why not try to live out the legacy of my royal ancestry and act accordingly?

I looked fresh the weekend after the fight at Ghoul's Park. Hollywood lent me his nugget, diamond-encrusted bracelet after I bugged him all week to let me wear it. He even dropped me off in his Mercedes. Southridge Senior's entrance was like any other high school's. It's where the popular kids congregated to be seen. The school entrance was like a catwalk. Everyone showcased their stuff. Girls gathered to see whose hot ride their friends were being dropped off in. The boys dropped off by the hustlers gained automatic notoriety. So my cruising in Wood's Mercedes-Benz made the girls stare. My gear was tight. I was the freshest kid at Southridge. The girls showed their appreciation. "Hey, sexy!" they hollered from the courtyard.

This was around the time when sisters weren't showing dark-skinned brothers love. They were more infatuated with Al

B. Sure and Chico DeBarge. A dark-skinned brother like me rocking a shaved bald head and getting love from the ladies made me hot stuff. I was a rebel of sorts.

Kim came running up to me. "Are we gonna hook up for lunch?" she whined.

Only if you let me tap that fat ass beyond the bleachers by the baseball field.

"I gotta see what my partners are up to first, lil mama," I answered.

The ladies dug me. I caught Kiesha out of the corner of my eye yapping with the evening-news crew. Every high school has that group of girls, gossiping about everybody. They know who the quarterback is giving it to as well as who came down with crabs. I didn't feel like being bothered.

"Maurice! We over here!" I heard someone yelling.

My crew was posted up by the water fountain near the courtyard. Construction crews were adding another classroom to the east wing of campus adjacent to the football field. The construction confined all the students to the courtyard and main hallway before classes started. This forced different crews who didn't particularly like one other to mingle in close quarters. That was an oversight on the part of school officials. Sure enough, I managed to bump into the boys I beefed with from Ghoul's Park. Lady Drama had a major crush on me. "What's up now, chump?!" the dude yelled. Folks called him T.

This guy couldn't be serious. His left eye was still swollen shut from the beating I gave him. The knot the Heineken bottle left on his forehead looked like a ripe tomato. I had to give it to this dude; he wasn't letting me off the hook that easy.

I shook my head. "You wanna die this time? Bruh, you

lucky my partners pulled me off of you the first go-around. Don't let your pride get you killed." I meant it.

He pushed me. Our crews started throwing punches, and the school erupted in mayhem. Now I was pissed. It wasn't enough for this guy to pick a fight with me without provocation on a cool weekend in the park. He had the nerve to ruin my first week of high school and the audacity to interrupt me while I was about to get my mack down! I gazed at the stack of plywood laid out where construction was taking place.

"What are you doing? Hey, are you crazy?" yelled one of the workers running behind me. Before he could grab me, T was laid out unconscious in the courtyard. I hit him so hard with that block of wood it cracked.

"Oh, shit!"

In minutes I was in a paddy wagon.

21

Money and Drugs

It was over. The Miami-Dade public school sys-
tem tried. They washed their hands free of me. I was a degen-
erate, mindless, uncontrollable street thug. T's family didn't
press charges, and no students would admit to seeing me hit
him. I was let go but permanently expelled from school. In
fact, if I was within one hundred yards of Southridge I could
be arrested.

I was relieved. I didn't fit in anyway. If the schools don't take
a young brother, the streets sure will. The dope boys will em-
brace a wayward kid with open arms. In that warped moment in
my life the streets seemed like the better option.

"Damn, bruh, they say you brought out the National Guard
at Southridge," joked Wood when he saw me later that week.

I wanted to ask a favor of Wood. I'd been burning to ask him since the first day I moved down here.

"Well, bruh, let me take you out to get your mind off of shit," Wood said.

The favor had to wait. Wood was going to take me to Strawberry's. After Biggs went down so did Heart of the City. Strawberry's was the new spot. All the shot callers went there. Professional athletes from out of town frequented the place. It was the grown-up nightclub. Pac-Jam over on Twenty-seventh Avenue was for teenagers, but Wood carried weight in the city. No bouncer in Miami was crazy enough to tell Wood where he couldn't go. That evening he took out a stack of thousands and we hit the town. When we pulled up to Strawberry's, the crowd was gracious, to say the least.

"Looking good, baby boy," said one bouncer. He gave Wood daps.

I was a duck out of water, but I followed suit. Inside, the deejay spun the latest records. Hip-hop had just started to rock in the club. Our resident hip-hop ambassador, Luther "Uncle Luke" Campbell, was putting our flavor to the music. Strawberry's was his club. Our women liked to get loose, so to speak. Folks in Miami like to get freaky, period. No one stood by the walls looking like statues. In our clubs people got down like a bunch of horny bastards. Luke threw a bunch of parties in Miami. He was the most well-known promoter. That's how he got his start in the music game. He brought all the big acts to Miami to get it popping. He was the first hip-hop mogul, but never gets his due credit. Before Memorial Day weekend's urban beach week, thousands of people flocked to Overtown Come Alive. Miami Bass music got started in clubs like Miami

Nights, Studio 183, and Strawberry's. Miami Bass got the boo-
ties shaking, and clubs around America followed suit. Alongside
Luke, other pioneers were rocking out clubs. Uncle Al, Sugar
Hill DJs, Prince Rahiem, Disco Rick and the Dogs, Le Juan
Love, Crazy Legs 59, Clay D, and Half Pint had also set the
tone of the Miami music scene. JT Money and the Poison Clan
were the first group in Miami in which each member rapped.
All of the previous acts added to Miami's unique sound.

That night I saw Wood talk with the owner and converse
with the deejay. Like I said earlier, dope slinging was temporary.
Hollywood didn't plan on being a dope boy all his life. He was
stacking his bread, hoping to open a club and get into the music
business. Every hustler knew the life expectancy of the coke life
was short. Hustlers don't live too long. Don't be fooled by the
Steven Seagal flicks. You will get touched in those streets.

I observed Wood when he was making those moves. He
wanted out bad. Hanging at Strawberry's and all the other nightclubs was as much business for Wood as pleasure. That night
while we cruised home, he turned up NWA. Those brothers Ice
Cube, Dr. Dre, DJ Yella, MC Ren, and Eazy-E were from a city
far away in California that we had never visited, but when they
spit those raps, we felt it all the same. Their music got to our very
souls. Luke's booty-shaking hits got the club crunk. We loved it
of course. Luke was our hip-hop godfather. Who could get mad
at a guy who had the ladies turning tricks and "popping coochie"
in the club?

Luke was also one of the few people back then outside of
the drug dealers who tried giving back to the community. Luke's
peewee football league saved a lot of young lives. Luke was
definitely one of the heroes in Miami's inner city. However, his

music catered to the raunchy side of things. He was catching hell from the U.S. government, who thought his songs were too vulgar and risqué for the American public.

Outside the club in Miami's streets we were really feeling that "fuck the police" type of music. *Straight Outta Compton* spoke to every black man in America. West Coast and Southern brothers had a lot in common. The music we generate is more laid-back and party-friendly than the music emanating from the concrete jungle where our brothers up North reside. However, I loved Kool G Rap. His music was believable. Miami's inner city was the grittiest in America, so we wanted that gutter music.

Wood used to ride around bumping the hard-core shit all day. It was the sound track to the lives we were living. But Wood's favorite emcee wasn't on the radio. *I* rapped for fun. "Bruh, I'm telling you that you can spit. You can rap, bruh," said Wood. "I can hear you on one of these records."

"Nah, bruh. Those boys are the truth. I just kid around," I fired back.

Word had spread throughout the projects that Wood's wild young brother was also the best with the pen and pad. Rapping was the only other thing I did well besides busting heads. Crews gathered in Richmond Park and threw their best lyrical jabs at each other. It usually started with jokes about the opponent's mother. My competition had way more material to throw at me than I did. That's actually how I learned to become extremely witty with my rhymes. I used the food-stamp and welfare insults and turned them into jokes about myself. Neutralizing the competition's ability to tear me down left them with no ammunition. After emptying my opponents own lyrical clip, I ripped them to shreds. I enjoyed it. So did my crew. They were even getting paid off my rap battles in the park by placing bets.

My rhymes were always ahead of my time. I was rapping from the perspective of the older G's I idolized, and it made the competition fear me. They were rapping about girls and fly kicks. Meanwhile, I'd hit them with:

Nigga know me from way back in the days / before rapping nigga I was selling crack in the day / before trapping nigga I was still packing that AK.

People were coming from far and wide throughout Miami to battle me. It was too easy. They started off with the usual "your mama broke and on welfare in the projects" jargon. Unknown to me, Wood was lining up emcees for me to devour.

He planned to take his record-label ambitions to a Gordy level. Our father had used his hustling money to start Suntown Records, the first label of its kind in Miami. But prison brought an abrupt end to it. Hollywood was betting on larger success with Ted "Touche" Lucas. My father had taken Ted under his wing so to speak. He showed him the ropes in the music business. Ted looked up to Hollywood, so when he came up with the idea to start pushing their own acts, Ted followed suit. The first group they signed was an R&B group called Nu Vibes. I believed Wood saw me as the true face of the fledgling label because on the ride home that night he was trying to convince me to become an emcee.

"Bruh, ain't nann nigga cold as you with this rap shit," he said. "All we gotta do is get you exposure. We gotta get you up there onstage."

I was never a shy kid but I thought those musical types were soft. All the money in the world couldn't get me on a stage, glistening like Snow White and doing dances. Strutting and posing wasn't part of my routine. I was too damn thugged out for that. Trading freestyles under the ficus tree in Richmond Park was one thing. Getting up onstage in front of thousands of people was an event I wasn't ready for. I always wanted to rap, but I didn't have the confidence to think anyone would take me serious.

"I'm just saying, bruh. You have something a lot of homeys out here don't have," Wood said. "You got options, bruh."

The only option I saw was the one that had made Wood such a superstar in the hood. I blurted out the favor I'd been burning to ask.

22

Bricks and Marijuana

"BRUH, LET ME HOLD THE WHITE."

The car screeched to a stop. Wood nearly blew a fuse. He was so mad I thought he was going to hit me.

"You out your fucking mind!" he yelled. "I been telling you about this rap shit and you wanna handle the work? Nah, bruh. Leave this shit alone. We're not out here doing this to look fly."

Wood's term to always "keep it one hundred" rang a bell. So many dope boys break down in those interrogation rooms on *The First 48* television show because that brother took on a life and wasn't ready to keep it one hundred. He knew the risk when he put his hands on that white girl. He knew it came with certain liabilities. If the decision ushered in the dark instead of the light, the code required the hustler to deal with it. Life was so hard in Miami it caused people to take on such risks.

Choirboys who started slinging dope for the hell of it, because of greed or the thrill factor, are the first to start giving up names. For every choice one makes in this world a consequence follows. I was ready to live within those parameters.

Wood gazed at me. I shook my head. He knew me by now. Those close to me began to understand that Maurice was going to do what he wanted to do. I was virtually on my own since I could walk. It was damn near pointless for anyone to tell me what to do now.

"It's grown-man business, bruh. There's certain rules to this shit. It ain't like when you were out there in the Beans flipping dollar joints," warned Wood. He tried; however, he knew I would find some way of getting to the powder. If it meant I had to jack some known hustler to do so, I was going to get to her. Wood shook his head.

Like I said before, the Miami River cops flooded the city with the stuff. Anyone could get their hands on bricks. Slinging coke was a profitable side business for a school-crossing guard. Pies use to go for between $40,000 to $50,000 in the days of Mundey and Roberts. Now anyone could get a pie for between $15,000 and $18,000 depending on who they knew. Cocaine suppliers were rogue dealers. Grocery-store managers and even the cop patrolling a neighborhood served packages. A random person sometimes drove by the strip and displayed bricks on his or her backseat. Those suppliers were like ghosts. No one knew who the hell they were connected to. He could have been the supplier himself. It was strategic on the part of someone's supplier to keep their customer in the dark on the whereabouts of the supply chain and price ranges and such. That's how they got rich while their middlemen did the dirty work. We were slaves to the supplier. Liberty City was a plantation ripe with cocaine as opposed to cotton. We were just some teenage niggas from the projects making them rich. These slave masters were some scary motherfuckers.

It was usually a Haitian or Cuban dude with no regard or respect for American life or its laws. A tourist wouldn't want to get lost in these cats' hoods while visiting the Caribbean. They were on a whole other level of carnage. As far as they saw it, American foreign policy had been bending their impoverished countries over without Vaseline for years. Making little Tommy a freebasing dope fiend was of no concern of theirs. Their plan was to make money in America and head back home with newfound wealth. Most were supporting families back in the islands with the proceeds. If black folks in America weren't wise enough to use the powder as a means to an end as opposed to getting fucked up on it, that was on us. They tried to school us along the way. As I mentioned earlier, they didn't take too kindly to taking crap from white folks. The chains of slavery had left the Caribbean way before they fell from our wrists.

Every time the cops would cruise by, those Jamaican hustlers would holler, "Bloodclot slavery ah finish, partna! I'll put two in a buoy, bloodclot head!"

I couldn't understand what they were saying, but I knew they weren't taking any shit. The Jamaican crew Shower Posse was one of the most insane crews to ever take up residence on U.S. soil. A Caribbean hustler's dope money was usually tied to a political cause so their motivation to sling was far more intense. They even displayed their wealth differently. They weren't flashy. Even with millions in foreign bank accounts, a beaten-down Land Cruiser was sufficient transportation. We spent our money on decked-out Cadillacs. There was a minor rivalry between us and the Caribbean and Latin gangsters, but we got past the language and cultural barriers when it was time to share the white girl. I guess we were stricken with jungle fever.

That night Wood studied me. He knew his younger brother was boarding a sinking ship. He hoped I'd jump overboard before it sank. People may say that Wood should have fought tooth and nail to keep me away from those streets. How could he? Hustling was in our DNA. The apple didn't fall far from the tree. It landed squarely at the root.

"I can't come behind you and clean up the milk you spill, bruh," Wood warned me. For all the love we shared, hustling was an individual trade. Any slick deals or shady business on my part might come back to literally kill him. In the streets, cosigning someone meant you bet your life on him. Another hustler would kill the snake as well as the person that put it in his midst. Wood knew he never had to worry about me snitching or the like. He feared my temper most.

"Bruh, you gotta pick your battles out here," he told me. "This ain't like the playground where a dude knocks you down and you heal. Ain't no coming back from a bullet to the head."

"These niggas can't see me bruh," was my foolhardy response.

He tried to warn me against it, but I went to Santana Red's warehouse. Santana was the man to see if any aspiring drug dealer wanted a piece of the white. I called up one of the older hustlers I knew was connected to him and we headed out.

23

Let Me Ride

HANGING AROUND WOOD MADE ME WANT THE LIFE he was living. I was the poor kid who hung around the rich hustlers and wanted what they had. Wood was dating quality girls. He was younger than the other hustlers, so mothers didn't mind him coming around their daughters. Innocent schoolgirl cherry is sure sweeter than some tired wench accustomed to being tossed around by gangsters.

Wood's main girl, Katrina, a majorette at Northwestern Senior High, was one such prize. Northwestern was the high school of high schools in Miami. All the fly chicks went there. Katrina was one of the flyest, ghetto yet classy in a Miami kind of way. I remember when Wood went to see her at the salon on Fifteenth Avenue where she and her mother did hair. Wood sure was getting the grade-A loving. The pleasures cocaine-pushing afforded a young brother were far too enticing. I couldn't wait to meet Santana Red.

Phantom. That's the best word I can use to describe the Cuban kingpin that supplied the bricks to young hustlers in the Beans. Rumors ran rampant that he was one of the exiles in the movement to overthrow Castro. People said he used the dope money to further his cause. It didn't matter to me. I knew he had the keys to heaven. I couldn't wait to get there. It felt as if we drove for an eternity before we finally reached Santana's outfit.

The abandoned warehouse sat out by the swamps in unincorporated Dade. The Everglades swallowed the area whole. I had passed the place before, but never took notice. Plenty of warehouses sat along the Florida Turnpike South on the way to the Miccosukee Indian Reservation. I guess Santana knew the Feds would never suspect it either. They were probably looking for him in some Coral Gables mansion. No one knew where the hell Santana stayed. The less one knows about a person, the more one fears him. Unfamiliarity keeps people at a distance, so they can't strategize an attack. The warehouse gave Santana a perfect vantage point to plan his attack. It offered him an unobstructed view for several blocks to see who was coming to conduct honest business or who was coming to rob or bust him. If someone was stupid enough to try the latter, it was their ass and the alligators. The Everglades is a wasteland. Except for rogue alligator-skin trappers, the place is desolate. A cry for help out there just fades into a haunting echo. If you die in those floating marshes, no one will ever find you.

We parked out by the dirt road leading to the turnpike.

Santana planned to meet us a couple hundred yards up ahead. The old-timer was methodical. He left no stone unturned. As we walked, his silhouette appeared, growing brighter as we drew closer. Then Santana stopped in his tracks.

"*Mi amigo*, what's this?" Santana said, gazing in my direction.

"No, it's cool. He's Wood's people," my friend answered.

"*Hermano es de Hollywood?*" said Santana, looking surprised. "*Señor Hollywood y familia* likes my business."

The older hustler who took me to meet Santana could have given me several of his own bricks to flip, but, like I said, dope hustling is an individual choice. I wanted to be my own man. I'm sure he consulted with Wood before taking me. They probably hoped such an introduction would scare me off. It didn't.

I soaked it all in. The coke life is addictive indeed.

Santana gave me one brick to drop. If I made a quick flip in the streets, I would get more. I was insulted. He was treating me like I needed a babysitter. I tried protesting before my guide pulled me away.

"Just make it drop, bruh," he said.

I did. I got the brick on Monday and gave Santana his cash Tuesday night. I may have been subpar in the classroom, but in the streets I was definitely an A student. My work ethic stemmed from the fact that I saw immediate results. The academic route was too long and offered nothing more than an uncertain future. I was tired of being piss-poor in the Beans. I wanted my cash now.

The rewards from drug dealing were instantaneous. I didn't see that train bearing down on my ass from miles away. I was living in the here and now. There wasn't any waiting for a check to clear. The money is tax-free. They say money can't make a person happy, but all that nice stuff it affords surely can make some of the things that make you unhappy disappear. I wanted my crew to reap the benefits as well. They were already hustling small-time. Like me, they had sold weed here and there. I always had a bit more than them because Hollywood kept me laced, but we were all broke the same. Convincing them was easy, and soon all of our fingers were stained with cocaine residue.

We weren't the only ones getting to the powder though. The strip of Fifteenth Avenue between Sixty-second and Sixty-fifth streets had become a catwalk of zombies and the dealers who fed them. The Beans had literally become a cracked-out dope town. A dope hole was on every corner. Traffic was routinely backed up by customers waiting to get their fix. The scene was more like an open-market food fair. Each dope hole was named after the hustler or the drug that was sold there. Addicts knew where to go to get that Criss Cross or Kilimanjaro. Kids sat perched out on the Twelfth Parkway as spotters. If narcs came crashing down the block, they sounded the alarm. Some dope boys paid the cops patrolling the strip to avoid the hassle. Everyone was on the crack payroll. For the right price a cop sat and watched your stash while you ran an errand. They passed the time getting served by schoolgirls on their way home from school. Those crooked cops used blackmail and all sorts of other tactics. A lot of kids in the Beans had parents with outstanding warrants. It was an easy pitch for cops.

You wouldn't want me taking your daddy down to central bookings, would you? It wasn't out the ordinary to see a patrol car parked on one of the side streets behind the projects rocking back and forth. After several minutes a teenage girl would emerge, disheveled and embarrassed before shuffling down the avenue with her head down. At times those cops took turns with the dope fiends. That's how hookers paid rent, so to speak, for working the officer's assigned zones.

Santana used Officer Tubbs to make deliveries. The first time that fat bastard pulled up to my crew in the park, I thought my burgeoning coke-trafficking career was over. He parked several yards away from the bench where we were posted and waved me over. I told Dante to use some of our rainy-day funds to bond me out of jail later. Everyday folks ride around with spare tires. Dope boys keep bond money on standby. It wasn't out of the ordinary. Those cops took pride in the mental games they played. They could have warrants on the passenger seat and cuffs ready to haul all of our asses down to jail, but that was too easy. They toyed with you first. Sometimes they had nothing on a kid at all. They were just bored. Sometimes, though, we toyed with them and made those cops look like circus clowns.

One time, the jump-out boys pulled up in unmarked cars outside Ghouls Park where I'd just started hustling, and we led them on a wild goose chase. My crew knew the side streets and alleyways like the alphabet. The gate in front of the alley that ran behind Dante's house was our favorite booby trap. So much hustling was going on back then the police force just let any old buster enlist, because the cops weren't too bright. The powers that be hadn't learned from the Miami River Cops fiasco. The jokers chasing us were seriously out of shape, gasping and wheezing within minutes of running behind our narrow behinds. Picture Humpty Dumpty chasing Speedy Gonzales.

"You got the right to an ass-whupping when I catch you,

nigga!" they yelled behind us. "Y'all lil niggas think this shit is a game!"

We let them give chase until we reached the entrance to the alley. The gate was put in place to keep cars from using the narrow strip as a shortcut. With no streetlight, a number of assaults had occurred there. We knew how to jump the gate without landing in the thorny brushes surrounding it. Catch-n-keep is what the Caribbean folks called the prickly weed that grows in the wild down here. It's a painful predicament for the unlucky soul who gets tangled in it. The posts the fence had been positioned on were cracked in half. We timed our jumps perfectly so we didn't put too much pressure on the fence. Then we pretended to slow down, even cramp up, just to entice them.

"Yeah, look at you now! I'm about to whup that ass! You think you can run from the police! Just wait till—"Aaaaaah! Aaaaaaah! Help!"

The screams coming from that officer facedown and all distorted in that patch of catch-n-keep was worth the adrenaline rush. Seeing him all bruised and distorted was gratifying. In seconds he was the laughingstock of everyone who hung out around the alley.

"Lay off the donut, sucker! Maybe you'll catch me next time!"

We taunted those cops until we disappeared around the block. It was temporary respite, a small victory in the face of the usual outcomes from our collisions with the police in Miami.

Ironically, those subpar cops wouldn't have had jobs if I wasn't out committing crimes. If everyone lived by the book, there wouldn't be a need for prosecutors, public defenders, judges, correctional officers, and cops. That's why the system backs some people into a corner. You don't need a justice system if you don't have crime.

For the most part there were no drug raids in the Beans. Dealers were slinging crack in broad daylight. Tubbs was just an opportunist trying to fit in. But he wasn't as crafty as Officer Smith and the Wire Tap Squad. Smith took what the River Cops did to a whole other level. Even the dealers he ripped off had to give him props for the sheer genius of his scheme. Smith figured out a way to rip off hustlers with limited or no violence. His crew listened in on conversations local dealers had with their out-of-town suppliers, then offered the dealers more favorable splits on the product. When the supplier came in to Miami, Smith had his crew emerge on the scene. They arrested Smith, but allowed his supplier to flee. Then the crew laughed all the way to the bank. Instead of turning in the evidence they sold it to the dealers. Feeling they dodged a bullet, the suppliers didn't realize they were actually being ripped off. Damn, that was some cold, hard shit.

It's why kids in Miami hated the police. Don't get me wrong, there were and still are some officers out there striving to make a difference in the community. Some believe that giving a young brother a pass and hooking him up with a work release program instead of sending him to the chain gang is better for everybody. Those idealistic types are few and far between, but crazy as it seems, I tried to understand where a cop like Tubbs was coming from.

An officer's salary sucked. Cops were out in these streets getting shot at by teenage dealers who had flashier rides than they did and were getting girls that looked like the ones cops saw in magazines. Then if that overworked officer did score a big bust, some pretty-boy district attorney held a press conference and took all the credit. That reality made for some bitter and corrupt officers.

As I approached his car, I could see that Tubbs had his pistol sitting in his lap. He was rolling several bullets in his hand. I had some crack rocks in my pocket, but wasn't concerned. It wasn't enough dope for him to go through the hassle of booking me.

"You're that little nigga they call Head?" he asked.

"Yeah, that's me," I said.

The more direct you were with cops, the quicker the mind fuck would end. It's not wise to aggravate an already miserable soul. Furthermore, Tubbs knew it was damn near suicide for me to be out in broad daylight talking to him where everyone could see. I wanted to keep this short and to the point.

"Look, you're about to arrest me or what?" I said.

"Maybe I am and maybe I'm not. All you're gonna do is stand there and look stupid until you figure it out, motherfucker," he fired back. "Yeah, you're Wood's little brother. You're Pearl's son. Your old boy is in the Feds."

I had visions of stabbing his fat ass and leaving him leaking all over the park, but Wood told me I had to pick my battles, and I needed to be mindful of that. However much of a lowlife, Tubbs was part of the machine, that well-oiled American justice system that took pride in destroying young brothers' lives. I let Tubbs continue his prodding.

"Look, there's nothing I would like more than to haul your young ass to the country. Better yet, I'd love you to get slick so I can cap you. The world would be better without you little nigga degenerates."

I was boiling inside.

"But the man say you're holding down the white lady pretty well." Tubbs motioned to the backseat. A brown paper bag was on the floor. I reached in, grabbed it, and started to walk off.

"Aren't you forgetting something, my nigga?"

I paused to mull his question over in my mind. A bell rang. I reached in my pocket and handed Tubbs a $100 bill. Before I could say something, he sped off, damn near running me over.

Tubbs was truly one low-down cop. Word on the street was that dope boys were paying him to serve warrants to rivals. But if Tubbs found out that rival had more loot to spend, Tubbs would flip the script on the dealer who approached him and arrest him instead. He was always setting up dudes for the fall. He offered his services to the highest bidder and was loyal to no one. Those Miami streets bred some messed-up individuals. My crew ran up to me. We opened the bag. Inside, our future lay stacked in neat, pearly white columns. I nearly fainted. At least ten pies were in that bag.

24

Who's Selling

IT WAS TIME TO GET OUT THE PARK AND OUT THIS nickel-and-dime hustle. We had to get our own corner. It meant loading up. The pistols we were packing weren't going to cut it if we were really going to start pushing coke on a major level. We had to fend off the obvious threats from rivals. Having a brick in Liberty City was like having the only canteen of water in a crowded desert.

The brick made you a target. Back then, dope boys rode around in Chevys with AK-47 and AR-15 assault rifles. They were living the same life as those Cuban and Colombian cats in the early eighties. If a rival dope boy caught you without your fire, that was on you. Miami's streets exceeded the mayhem in

John Wayne's wildest westerns. From Opa-locka to Ghouls and all hoods in between, dope boys were setting the streets ablaze.

As dope crews battled over turf in Miami, the streets remained stained in blood. The Beans was prime real estate. That's where the smokers grazed. The rest of Miami went on with their day-to-day amid the sunshine while my corner of the city died a slow, crack-induced death. "I got that good green brown! Boulders, boulders!"

Dealers sought customers around the clock. If a smoker overdosed, word spread like wildfire. That dope hole had the good stuff. Smokers would rush that dope hole like a moth to the bulb. We held Liberty City's street corners hostage.

Folks drove into the Beans from the suburbs, Fort Lauderdale, and other parts of the county just to get high. Liberty City offered one-stop shopping for all vices. If a customer wanted a blow job while he snorted some lines, we had that. Everything was for sale. Sadly, though I didn't know this then, we were also selling our humanity. Pushers didn't discriminate on who could buy nickel rocks. Pregnant women. Grandmothers. Schoolkids. If customers had the money, they could suck their life away on a crack pipe.

Staking out a corner for my crew didn't prove difficult. I was raised in the Beans. Furthermore, I was still tight with Darryl and O'Sean, who were now moving major weight. At first there wasn't much beefing going on because everyone respected the rival dope boy's hole.

The Haitians had fought to gain their street credibility and did. When they first moved to the area in Liberty City known as Little Haiti during the late 1970s, we gave them hell. We bought into the hype mainstream American media was selling, like blaming them for bringing AIDS to America, and found ourselves fighting with the Zoes. Later I would learn that Haitians were the first black folks in our part of the globe to gain independence from white folks. They kicked the French out. No wonder the world is still giving them a hard time. A nigga that comes out on top is a hard pill to swallow for most folks. However, the global support Haiti received after the recent earthquake shows that the powers that be may finally be making reparations for the bad hand dealt to that country.

Colonizers have always pitted colored folks against each other. It's called divide and conquer. The media reports made us believe that the newly arriving Haitians had diseases and worshipped Satan. African-Americans bought into the lies, and soon enough we were battling with Haitians like pit bulls in a dog pound. Haitian kids were afraid to say they were from Haiti. They were getting jumped and beaten all throughout Liberty City. It was safer for Haitians to say they were from Jamaica or the Bahamas. So they formed a crew called the Zoe Pound to protect themselves from attacks from other black folks. Zoe in Creole means "bone." And those dudes were hard as bones. When a Haitian kid was being picked on, the Pound would seek out the culprit and retaliate. It's like I said: niggas don't like niggas.

That crew was and still is one of the coldest crews in Miami-Dade. Soon enough it became the season of the Zoes in Miami. They pushed the powder out of a dope hole called the White House. Some of the realest cats I know are Haitian. Visitors to Little Haiti can't peruse certain spots without a pass from the Pound. They did their thing over there while we did ours in the Beans. Black Zoe was at the helm. He was taken aback that the dope boys sometimes went to Santana Red for their dope instead of him when Zoe was short on supply.

"We are all African brothers," he used to say.

I know that pitch sounds crazy, but that was the crazy world I existed in. It was all about moving the coke. Everyone was desperate for money.

My crew set up shop and began serving smokers. At first no one beefed because every hustler was getting paid. This conglomerate had codes of conduct. Customers couldn't talk in the dope hole. Get your rocks and keep moving. The smokers knew which drug they wanted that day and sought it out, so there was minimum drama on their part. In the downtime, dope boys passed time playing craps. It was all gravy.

Tubbs cruised by now and again to see what was hot on the block. He was always scheming. He extorted his fair share of dope boys in his time. It's probably how he paid for his kids' college education.

My crew toiled day in and day out. We were making anywhere from $4,000 to $5,000 a night. It didn't come close to what Hollywood was making, but it felt good nonetheless. The more we stacked, the harder we hustled. That's the thing about coke money. I wanted more of it because it was coming in so easy. I also spent it as fast as I made it.

We stayed fresh. Ironically, a dope boy spends so much time trying to make more money that he doesn't make time to enjoy spending it. All the while I stacked my bread, others were waiting to take it from me. The same way we were preying on the weak, serving them their street medicine, someone was eager to prey on us.

In the criminal world, some prey on fellow criminals. Every industry has its share of opportunists.

Enter the jack boys.

25

Kill-a-Head

You have to be one cold or downright crazy dude to make a living robbing hustlers. It's not like stealing from the guy working the register at 7-Eleven. Nevertheless, some had a twisted enough mental disposition to become stickup kids, like the boys from Lincoln Fields.

It's safe to say we spent summers trying to kill one another. Lincoln Fields was the projects across the parkway, a mere three blocks away from the Beans, but judging from the amount of gunfire we exchanged, those cats might as well have been Al Qaeda. PSU projects were also around the way, but for the most part they got along with crews in the Beans.

I'm sure all of us shared common roots, but the coke tore us apart. Some days folks stayed in for fear of catching a stray bullet when we shot at one another. Shell casings littered the block. Bullet holes were everywhere. People huddled in their bathtubs with their kids when they heard the sound of gunfire. They laid on the floor and waited until the AK spent its magazine.

Being the new kids on the block made us targets, and in time the Lincoln Fields crew made a move on us.

"Y'all seen that black Impala coming round all the time?" said this one kid we paid as a lookout.

"Ain't nothing we can't handle, bruh," I would say.

We kept our rifles in an old Chevy we drove around. We hadn't graduated to the candy-painted dunks the more successful dope boys drove. A dunk is what we called a Chevy Impala or similar car. Their dunk had spinning rims with a cocaine-white interior. If a hustler was riding in a '71, '72, or '73 dunk, he was doing big things. We kept our car parked on the curb in front of the dope hole with someone lounging in it in case anything went down. If so, we were ready to lock and load.

I have to give it to those Lincoln Field dudes. The first time they rolled up on us, they caught us totally off guard. I was lounging in the car bumping the radio while some dope boys were being entertained by Mr. Jingles, a smoker who had a fondness for Sammy Davis Jr. and danced like it was showtime at the Apollo. From the way he moved, Jingles could have performed on Broadway, instead of tapping his heels on Fifteenth Avenue. As Jingles moved into a new routine, a smoker started giving our lookout a hard time. I sat back and observed. I had seen the addict before. He was a regular so I didn't pay him any mind.

"I told you don't come around trying to sell T-shirts!" the lookout yelled. "You're making the spot hot."

The smoker had wheeled a shopping cart filled with old VCRs, stereos, and other junk right up onto the curb. We didn't mind the guy getting his hustle on, but he needed to sell his junk and move on. The stuff was probably stolen, so the police were sure to come snooping around.

"Keep it moving, partna," said Tronne, getting up from his chair under the tall ficus tree.

"Y'all ain't the only ones trying to earn a living out here," said the smoker. "I'll give you this VCR for a dime hard."

Everyone looked him up and down as if he was crazy. This dude wanted a whole dime for some rusted VCR. Crack really messes with the brain. I continued bumping my tunes. Then the smoker freaked, flipped his cart over, and started stomping up and down like a lunatic.

Our spotter reached for his pistol. "I said back up before I light your bitch ass up!" the kid screamed.

Still, I wasn't moved. Some dealers had started stretching the dope with all kinds of chemicals so they could turn higher profits. Sherm, cush, premo, and the other drugs that resulted really had smokers bent out of shape at times. I kept bumping to Le Juan Love. Then I caught a glimpse of the shooter bearing down on us. He was running up from the alley behind Sixty-fourth Street where the vacant field separated Lincoln Fields from Fifteenth Avenue. I reached for my AK on the backseat, cocked it, then opened fire.

The first time you see death bearing down on you, time freezes. Imagine a movie stopping on a single frame, music reduced to the loud thumping of your own heart. In that pause, all of the various scenes in your life explode into an awkward twilight of pure reaction.

You do or you don't.

Bullets ripped through the avenue. The corner-store windows shattered. People ran screaming. If that dude was going to kill me, I wanted at least one of my bullets to hit him. My life wasn't worth shit, but he couldn't send me to sleep untouched.

"Those niggas shooting! Someone call the police!"

I ducked on the ground beside the car as I fired. Our lookout had already sped off on his bicycle. The shooter returned fire from behind a lamppost at the intersection. The black Impala banked the corner. The shooter jumped in. My crew piled in our Chevy and gave chase up Twelfth Parkway. I leaned out the passenger-side window shooting.

They had underestimated my crew and were now just trying to get away. Dante was leaning out the back window firing as well. Tronne was busy loading his clip with one hand on the steering wheel. We chased them all the way to Seventh Avenue before we heard police sirens and bailed.

I wanted to kill them. I wanted them stuck in the ground. I wanted to inflict on them the pain I suffered on the inside. I guess that's what psychiatrists call projection. We project onto others the issues we're dealing with. But I had another way of coping with my demons.

26

So High

Interview any smoker in Miami who copped my drugs back in the day. The consensus will be that I had the good white. Maurice's stuff got smokers to that high they were looking for all week. It wasn't just because I cared. I was using my product. I broke the first rule from the dope boy's handbook and was getting high as a kite on my own supply. Pills, coke, crack, and all sorts of other drugs were helping me race through the madness that was my life. I valued the product I sold.

When cats that never used dope started slinging, they had no appreciation for the product. They didn't understand just how much a good high meant when you hit rock bottom, so they added all kinds of chemicals to the drugs. They started remixing it. I could relate to my customers. I was their number one dope boy. We were all sleeping with the same bitch. No one got jealous. It was an open relationship of sorts.

My favorite was boonk.

I'd get 7 Cents weed from the Jamaicans and pack it in a blunt. I separated the seeds. You don't want to burn those. Then I sprinkled some coke over it. I sealed that sucker and puffed. In that one toke all my problems went away. I was numb to the fact that I was permanently thrown out of the public school system. My resentment toward my father subsided. The projects didn't seem so hopeless anymore. The piss scent that permeated from the curb was masked. All my worries went up in smoke. But the habit also made me more reckless than ever.

Word spread fast that my crew was on some Rambo shit. Every hood has its wildest pack of wolves. We were that crew. Folks started calling us the Get High Boys because of the bomb dope we sold. Rivals couldn't even drive by us with a cold stare. We opened fire without thinking. After all, I was Trick. That's what my friends started calling me. Coming up in the hood, everyone had a nickname. The label was usually something that made you stand out. In our opinion the government name your parents gave you was just some title to get by in society's good graces. Maurice sounded good on a résumé. Trick embraced the street life. I added *Daddy* at the end because my friends said even though I was young, I acted like an OG.

The reputation came with a price. We were some young cats so the notion that we were really that hard-core rubbed some older dudes the wrong way. Then, some crews our age thought they were just as hard. In the hood it's never good to front like you're the hardest. Someone will always be lurking, ready to bring out the sweetness in you. That challenger decided to rob Wood's mother. He went further than robbing her though. He outright disrespected her. "If I had time, I would fuck you, with your fine ass," he told her. Since most boys in the hood grow up with single mothers, disrespecting someone's old girl is off-limits. It's like making a death wish.

The situation is ironic to say the least, given the way the terms *bitch* and *ho* are tossed around the hood so freely. Ghetto politics can be warped and twisted I guess. That's how the mama jokes in the hood started. Someone would say, "Your mama is so fat, she looks like her pants are on steroids," or, "Your mama smells so bad the Pine-Sol dude follows her around." Insulting someone's mother was the easiest way to get that person riled up. It was also the easiest way to get killed.

A week later at a house party we saw the same guy who robbed Wood's mother. He was posted on the wall talking to a shone. Wood sent his friend Bobby over there.

"Hey, bruh!"

"Come here for a second!"

The guy jetted.

He ran out the back, then broke through the gate at the entrance to Rainbow City projects. Just like that his happy evening turned into the run of his life. We jumped in Wood's Chevy convertible and sped after him. The car screamed down the avenue. He ran like a man possessed.

"Run, nigga, run! Run for your life, bruh!"

Shouts came from people spilling out the projects. Parents grabbed their kids from getting caught in the melee. We were now only several yards away. The guy turned to catch a glimpse of the car bearing down on him. The Chevy slowed to a creep. Wood reached for his rifle and aimed, then let the birds fly.

As we sped off, the guy was slumped on the curb in a pool of blood. As we saw it, he had no business disrespecting Wood's mother. Back then, the consequences of taking a life never really weighed heavy on our psyches. People in my neighborhood acted before they thought. No one contemplated the what-ifs. When tomorrow repeats like the same sorry yesterday, people end up existing only within the moment. *Right now this nigga crossed the line, so he gotta die. No ifs, buts, or maybes. Fuck him and the life of his sorry-ass family.* I didn't stop to think that a simple apology could have rectified the situation. Lives got thrown away over words and angry glances. We died silly in the hood. But he *lived.*

When he left the hospital weeks later, the bullets hadn't slowed him down. A couple of shots to his chest and legs didn't convince him it was time to reform his bad-guy habits. This dude was determined to keep on keeping on. The day he left the hospital he went to Wood's mother's house looking for Bobby. The neighborhood was throwing a block party. Those parties are where people got crunk.

The resident deejay spun the latest Disco Rick, Prince Rahiem, Crazy Legs, and Luke. Our deejays back then weren't like the ones spinning today. They weren't driving expensive cars and living like celebrities. He was usually some brother hustling in the street and spinning records as a hobby, as a way out. The deejay was an icon in the hood, an integral part of our culture. Uncle Al was one of the many neighborhood favorites.

Guys like Al were musical pioneers before rappers. They freestyled over someone's record. They introduced storytelling and rhyming over other people's beats before there was such a thing as a mixtape. The story was usually about an everyday experience. Then the deejay took the record and added extra bass to it.

Outside Wood's mother's house that weekend the scene mirrored a typical block party. Two giant Lazy Boy speakers were posted outside on the corner. The music could be heard five blocks away. The mood was gravy and everyone was jumping, until the guy Wood shot caught sight of Bobby.

He rushed Bobby and pistol-whipped him. He pounced on Bobby like a priest on the devil on Judgment Day. The party turned to mayhem. People were jumping over chairs to get to their cars. The deejay pulled the plug on the tunes and joined the stampede. A fight like this was inevitable at one of the parties Wood's mother threw. There were just too many people and too much liquor for a peaceful evening. Liquor and niggas don't mix like a hog's ass and perfume. Sure enough somebody gets angry and decides to shoot the place up. And that's exactly what the guy who Wood shot did.

That's why I knew we should have made sure that dude was dead that day. Wood knew when we fired on that dude repercussions would follow. Pride and manhood are jewels, stolen from black boys at birth. The best way we know how to regain that self-esteem is by destroying the first thing that challenges it. I've seen kids die over stepping on another man's sneakers. After Bobby recovered from his pistol-whipping, fate dealt him a worse hand. Some cops shot him more than thirty times over a drug deal gone bad. I told you those Miami cops were ruthless.

The number of incidents with crews testing me escalated. If a rival didn't like me, he found a way to create drama with me. There is no such thing as avoiding beef in the hood. If I turned the other cheek, my challenger would definitely have smacked it. Then I would forever be getting my ass kicked. Something as simple as a rival saying he didn't like me staring at him could lead to a shoot-out. Even if my neck was in a brace and I was forced to look his way, he would have used that as the spark. Imagine playing basketball and an opponent says you fouled him too hard and smacks you in the mouth when you simply tried to block his shot. Soon enough you'd either have to learn to fight or pick up and move to Pinecrest or some other ritzy suburb. I couldn't afford to move to Pinecrest so I was stuck staring down his sorry ass.

The confrontations should have slowed me down. There's no pension fund or 401(k) for a dope slinger. There are only two possible endings to look forward to: a patch in the graveyard next to an enemy or a life sentence in a cage contemplating. I've visited the cemetery and seen a friend's tombstone resting a yard away from one of his adversary's. Life is ironic indeed. He couldn't stand the brother in this world. Now their bones wrestled it out in the dirt for eternity. Their souls will forever haunt the cemetery with their bickering.

I couldn't see that dead end up ahead though. I was racing down a lonely one-way strip, liquored up, high on cocaine, and out of my mind. First, I started speeding through yellow lights. Now I was racing through red ones. The flashing lights in my rearview signaling for me to slow down were only minor distractions. There were signs that the streets were devouring us whole.

No one on the block had seen Big Black or Shrimp in months. Then word finally got around: Black and Shrimp had caught a charge, murder. Word on the street was that they both got 137 years with a life sentence. At 15, my friend's life had already ended before it began. I kept on hustling, praying fate would deal me a better hand.

27

You Never Know

AT 8 A.M. ON APRIL 3, 1991, THE FRONT GATE OUT-
side Richmond Heights Middle School was packed with kids in
green and yellow on their way to first period. Teachers rounded
up stragglers under the sprawling ficus trees that lined the
courtyard. I always daydreamed when I pulled up to that gate.
Those kids looked so *free,* as if they were living in some kind of
real-life fairy tale. Their days weren't scripted by police chases
and shoot-outs. They were doing kid things. I watched them
exchange little love notes, the kind with two boxes sketched at
the bottom that comes after the most life-changing inquiry for
any adolescent: Do you like me? It's the question that makes
childhood special. I'd gotten butterflies in my stomach after
the girl whose pigtails I'd been pulling all year finally checked

yes. That's the boy-meets-girl, coming-of-age, growing-pains tale most people tell their grandkids. Those kids in the courtyard talked about who's taking who to the skate party. At lunchtime I'm sure they shot marbles behind the gym. The only mischief before heading to football practice was probably spitball fights in class. *What if?* I wondered.

"Can you put that out!"

Hollywood's sister Keba was yelling at me. She always hated the smoke. The scent that comes from mixing cocaine with weed is atrocious. It's a pungent, musty aroma that I learned to breathe in. The high, I felt, was necessary. At her age, she didn't understand that if I didn't smoke, I might lose the last screw holding my brain together. Keba needed to be protected from all the madness. Her world needed to be sketched in images of Barbie dolls and slumber parties.

"Oh, sorry, lil mama," I apologized, and let the tinted window down in the black Chevy Blazer—Black Beauty, that's what we called her—just enough so the smoke from my blunt could escape.

By now we were making so much money that my crew had graduated to trafficking. We made deliveries. Santana hooked us up with the Blazer. It wasn't anything fancy. It was inconspicuous, unlike the dunks with spinning rims and all that. The corners were getting too hot anyway. As I mentioned earlier, when bodies dropped, the jump-out boys came snooping around. Looking back, it's ironic we called that truck Black Beauty. The thing was an actual death deliverer.

One of our main spots to make deliveries was the Holiday Inn at Seventy-ninth Street and Seventh Avenue across from the I-95 expressway overpass. We called it the Carter Building. But not even Nino Brown had seen the amount of dope that used to run through that place. Whatever a customer wanted in the criminal world, he could find there. It's where criminals from out of town came to do their bidding. It was the UN building of the streets in Miami. Hookers, contract killers, and dope were all on standby at the Carter.

Either the coke we shuttled around the city would lead to a slow death or the AK-47s we had cocked on a moment's notice would blow a rival's back out. We were a dope supplier's dream; too young to get caught on any serious charges—we thought—and even more heartless than the average dope hustler. It was a simple but efficient drug-running operation. Drivers hopped out at various blocks so cops couldn't ID one particular trafficker. Narcs had put surveillance on the truck cruising the hood. They were definitely onto us, but they could never catch us with the dope when they pulled us over. The stops offered comedy as always.

"Good day, Officer. Ain't it just a nice sunshiny day out?" one of us would say.

The officer smirked. He tried hard to ignore our sarcasm.

We continued, "Damn, why y'all coppers always so bent outta shape. Oh, it's probably because all these little hoodlums out here causing all these problems."

"Y'all think this is one big joke, hunh?"

We wouldn't let up. "You know, I heard getting high calms the nerves. I don't know if it's true though. You know how people gossip in the hood."

Our truck usually smelled like marijuana or whatever other drug I was getting high on at the time. It was too small of a charge. These cops were after a bigger score. They had their eyes set on Santana. If they got lucky once and caught us with his product, they would try squeezing us to get to him.

Pistol-whip these little niggers. Ram their fucking heads into a windshield. We don't give a damn about these welfare cases. They're just pawns in a game of chess we're not going to lose to some wetback coke suppliers.

For all they knew, Santana or any other of the Caribbean cats supplying the white could have gone back to the islands. Those dudes weren't greedy. They were crafty in their dope slinging. Selling the powder served a larger purpose. Whether their funds were used as political leverage or to support families, those cats weren't going to let the American government win this *war.*

The officer would try to explain. "Y'all either too dumb or just blind to see where this thing is headed. You think that little gold chain or Jordans on your feet makes you the man?"

We did. You couldn't tell us we weren't the best thing since sliced bread. You would feel the same way if you grew up on government cheese, packed your holey sneakers with cardboard, and played hide-and-go-seek when the lights got turned off.

It still shocks me to this day what people call the land of the free. My question is, for whom? We have multimillion-dollar homes in Miami and homeless folks a stone's throw away on the other side of the street.

The only time I got a reality check that we were just pawns in a broken world was when we cruised down to South Beach on occasion. There wasn't anything down there for us. We were just bored I guess. Black locals in Miami rarely visit South Beach. The powers that be finally allowed our blacks to stay at the hotels, but it was a forced welcome. I have family members well into their sixties who've lived in Miami all their lives and have never been to South Beach. It sounds crazy, but there are club owners who'll use anything as an excuse to stop blacks from entering. They often say Dickies jeans or baseball caps aren't allowed, knowing damn well a white boy just walked in wearing the same thing. Hip-hop on South Beach was something new. Strawberry's, Miami Nights, Studio 183, and block parties were the few places to go to enjoy hip-hop. Since the mainstream started paying attention to our sounds, the club owners took notice.

I say fuck your ritzy nightclubs if I can't get in wearing my Dickies and fitted cap. The black people who frequent South Beach are most likely tourists or had just moved here. When my crew drove down there and stared at the half-naked spring breakers, they got fond of what folks might call our Southern swag.

"Lil Mama . . . Lil Mama! . . . What dey do?"

They giggled. I don't think they ever saw a Chevy sitting higher than three feet off the ground with spinners. Our gold grills were something out of the ordinary as well. We might as well have been from Mars. We turned right back around and headed on the I-395 causeway back to our side of the bridge. It wasn't as rosy, but it's where we felt comfortable. Gazing at all those yachts, sports cars, and mansions made me even more determined to be the best damn cocaine cowboy I could be. That cop's advice definitely fell on deaf ears.

28

Pull Over

THAT APRIL MORNING I HAD PLANNED TO SLEEP IN. There was work to be done later, but Hollywood had asked me if I could drop the girls off at school. As much as I wanted to, I couldn't say no. When Wood said ride, I rode.

I brushed my teeth, threw on my black T-shirt and short, black Dickies jeans. It's safe to say all I wore was black. Besides the gold glitter coming from my nugget bracelet, I was draped all in black, the color of a gangster. I'd like to clear something up. Cops kept harassing kids they saw dressed in all black. Word on the street was that cops believed a kid donning that color signaled that he was on the hunt to go wet somebody, that he was commissioned to kill someone. That's a pile of cattle shit. In my neighborhood folks would cap you whether they were dressed in pink, yellow, green, or aqua blue. Black is just a G thing.

I looked at my reflection in the bathroom mirror. The person staring back at me was *lost*. I had an oversize head resting between two pointy shoulders on top of a scrawny body. My appearance made me fodder for jokes. I wondered why I was born with such frailty in such a wild hood. If fate would have me born in the jungle, at least bless me with some size. I'm still only about 170 pounds sopping wet with bricks in my pocket. However, I made up for it. It made me bold.

Tater kept the engine running in Black Beauty, a '91 SUV, hollering, "Come on!"

I bolted out the door barefoot.

"Damn, bruh . . . took long enough," he fumed as I jumped in the passenger seat.

We called Dante, but he said he would catch up with us later after he met with his parole officer. The heat had been catching up to us for some time now. Dante had caught a charge.

"Relax, bruh . . . you got that boonk for me?"

There was no better breakfast than coke and weed.

"What you think?" replied Tater, unwrapping a plastic Ziploc bag with tiny packets of marijuana and cocaine. I unpeeled a Philly blunt and filled it with marijuana and coke before sealing it with saliva. With one light the blunt sparked. I reclined in my seat and turned the volume up. JT Money erupted from two Pioneer wood-grain speakers vibrating in the trunk. JT and the Poison Clan had some hot street records coming out of Uncle Luke's camp.

As the SUV cruised down Northwest Fifteenth Avenue, the corners where crews were already setting up shop were waking up. The work began while most of the rest of Miami slept. Crews dressed in the same black T-shirts and short, black Dickie jeans as me held positions at virtually every intersection along the avenue.

The spotters were getting their orange juice and ham-and-cheese sandwiches outside the corner bodegas farther up the block. As the coke brought more and more money, it offered opportunities even for the smokers themselves. When they wanted to go fraternize with a schoolgirl at lunchtime, the spotters gave a couple of dollars and nickel rocks to Lu Lu and One Eye, two neighborhood homeless cats, to guard the stash.

It took a while for those two jokers to realize some of those cops were suppliers themselves though. False alarms were routine. Since my crew graduated to making drop-offs, the younger dudes on the corner got crafty. Their stash was left in holes carved out in palm trees. It's ironic how everything in life evolves. The dope boy coming after you learns from your mistakes and becomes a bit craftier and more efficient. That's how trades are passed down through the generations. Dope slinging was a birthright in Liberty City.

The lookouts nodded while we cruised past that April morning. They peered inside the jet-black tint, daydreaming of riding inside one day. The corners were quiet. Fiends usually flocked the corners by sunrise after passing out from a good trip, but that morning the usual rush-hour line was down to two or three.

"It's dem boys from Lincoln Fields," said Tater, responding

to the frown on my face. We crossed Northwest Thirteen Avenue and there they were. Addicts huddled outside the Lincoln Fields blue-and-cream-colored low-rises just one block west of Fifteenth Avenue.

"This is ridiculous, bruh. I'm sick of these dudes, but I got the fire for them later. You just can't let someone take your corner. Next thing you know they're taking your house," I said. "Might as well let them bone your wife while they're at it."

We had already left those corners. I really had no stake in beefing with those guys. I was just more preoccupied with the principle of it. I didn't like them.

"Can y'all hurry up? We're gonna be late," whined Keba in the backseat. Her friend Chrystal was pouting alongside her.

Tater jumped out at the corner of Sixty-second Street to handle the work. I bolted onto the turnpike heading south toward Richmond Heights Middle. I sped through the neighborhood and crossed over to Seventeenth Avenue.

"Told y'all I'd make it on time," I said, turning to the girls.

In my childhood, there really wasn't much happiness. The playground scene in front of the school always offered me temporary respite from the bullshit. Flashing blue and red lights in the rearview forced me back into reality. I had whizzed pass the stop sign at the intersection.

"What's happening?" Keba asked.

"Don't worry, lil mama, we good," I told her. But sweat poured from my forehead as a female officer approached the Blazer. As I mentioned earlier, police in Miami had been watching the Blazer for months. They knew the truck. They knew what went down inside.

"You're in a hurry, young man?" the officer asked me.

"Kind of, Officer. I didn't want my lil sister to be late," I answered. The girls flashed a broad smile at the officer.

"Well, you sped past a stop sign in a school zone. That's not safe," the officer continued. "You girls go run along now. We wouldn't want you guys to be late."

She let the girls head to class and asked me to step out the vehicle. She patted me down. "No shoes . . . you were really in a rush, huh?" she joked.

I forced a smile. For some reason, Keba ran back to the car. She had forgotten her textbook on the backseat. Out of the corner of my eye I saw her freeze. She saw the nine-millimeter Walther PPK semiautomatic handgun tucked underneath her textbook where Tater had forgotten it. Her eyes locked with mine in the rearview mirror. She put the gun in a folder under her arm, then raced off. The officer gave me the usual lecture. She advised me to try to get my GED before writing a citation.

"Okay, looks like you're good," the officer told me. "Now go put some shoes on." She chuckled.

I got in the truck and banked the corner. Suddenly, I heard officers shouting. Keba was facedown on the pavement with guns drawn to her head.

29

Ten-Twenty-Life

KEBA, BEING THE HOTHEAD SHE WAS, GOT INTO AN argument with a classmate. In the melee, the gun had fallen from under her arm.

"Nah . . . leave her go . . . it's my gun!" I yelled as I raced back to the scene.

The officers handcuffed me and searched the truck. My heartbeat pelted against my chest.

We made that drop the other day. So I'm cool, these cops ain't got anything on me. They can book me for gun possession. I'll be out in the morning.

They reached for a laundry basket that was in the trunk. An officer smiled. He waved his partners over. Tucked in the laundry basket, wrapped in towels, they found three kilos of cocaine.

They hauled me down to that juvenile detention center once again. This time felt different though. No one had to tell me that my chances had run out. It's like gambling. I kept on playing the slots until I lost. It isn't rocket science. It's a game of probability. And the odds were telling me, *Not this time, buddy. You lose.*

All the trouble I had caused smacked me right in the face. I sat in the cell thinking about Fudge's lessons. I thought about Old Man Booner and Junior. Why didn't I listen? I was already getting beat up by regret, then Pearl and my stepmother showed up at the same time to get me out of the center. As much pain as I had caused Pearl, she never gave up on me. I gave up on myself. A mother's love is long-suffering. A mother is always the last person to leave her son's sentencing, the last one in the room when her kid's life is evaporating due to complications from AIDS after a life of drugs and prostitution. Mothers never give up on their kids. A bell goes off when their offspring is hurting. It rings when their baby boy is stressed-out during his final exam in college. Fathers aren't built with the same chip.

Son, I've carried you as far as I can. I've given you a map, but the rest of the journey is up to you. You've seen me suffer from the bullshit decisions I've made. Hell, that's how I ended up with you. Don't be stupid. God speed.

Isn't that messed up? Most black boys begin with a cracked compass. It points you south when you're supposed to be going north. Now you're stuck in the marshes with alligators looking at you crazy.

What, nigga? You're in our swamps. Don't get it twisted homey. You get a pass this time.

Pearl and Lynn showing up at the jail was a disaster waiting to happen. All hell broke loose. They began fighting and caused all sorts of mayhem. I must be the only juvenile in Miami-Dade history who got stuck in the detention center because the people coming to pick him up got into a fight. Pearl had lost custody of me and she wasn't having it. It didn't matter how rotten a seed Maurice Young had become. I was her rotten seed. But Mama couldn't save me now. I had to weather this storm alone. It's like Wood said. This is grown man's business.

I spent twenty-one days in lockup waiting for the courts to decide whom I should be released to. I sat there in that cell thinking my life was over. I used to bite at my fingers until the flesh bruised. My cellmate had to point it out before I noticed my bloody cuticles. All those times I fired my gun I wondered why I didn't get hit. The afterlife had to be better than this sorry one I was living. Surely my life couldn't have got any worse than it was already. I cried inside but no tears came. It did get worse.

He paid me a visit. I had seen this guy before. He was a white cat, rather portly fellow. He was at Santana's warehouse on occasion and often cruised the strip in his gray Porsche. He was never much for words, just stared at me like he knew something I didn't. Or at least that's the way he tried to come off, all serious and enigmatic. He wore an Armani suit like a glove. Maybe Italian or Jewish, I couldn't tell, but to a young kid in the Beans, a blue-suit-wearing white guy hanging with a Cuban dope king and kicking it in the Beans meant one of three things. He was either coming to the projects to get high, had a fixation for black hookers, or was the one calling the shots.

I was wrong. He was Santana's lawyer. My respect for Santana grew by the minute. That hustler came to America, got folks these sides all coked up, and had the white boy doing all his dirty work. He didn't strike me as a lawyer at first, but now it all made sense. He was hanging around the projects to keep watch over Santana's workers. Like I said, we were slaves on a cocaine plantation. We didn't know just how big America's crack problem was becoming. I had no idea the war reached beyond our street corners. Reagan put us up on that. America had put Manuel Noriega in Miami federal prison because of the powder. I think Noriega was using the drug proceeds to better his country. The U.S. government couldn't get a piece of the proceeds so they locked him up. It's all a game, and brothers get locked outside when the real decision makers are in the boardroom.

Santana's lawyer was a buffer. For a price he could bamboozle the justice system into an innocent verdict for Al Capone. He only came by to see if I was scared because Santana thought I may have snitched. I was a dead man walking if I did. At my age it was easy for me to crack. The cops already had me in that interrogation room. They played bad-cop, good cop. "Look, kid, we know the coke ain't yours. You were just out there trying to take care of your family." The soft approach was routine. "I grew up in the same projects. I know how it is."

Do you? Do you know how it is to walk with holes in your shoes until your feet blister where jigga worms reside? The other kids at school call you Pearl's food-stamp baby. You shoot at boys who look like you because these realities make you hate yourself. No disrespect, Officer, but things sure have changed since you left the Beans.

They offered me McDonald's and any other treat they thought would sucker me into giving up the man, but they had already lost the war. The powder had given kids a chance even if the outlook was bleak. I sat there for hours and ignored their advances.

"Did you know the dope was bad? Did you know your fairy godfather was ripping you off?"

I smirked, a rare show of emotion.

"Oh, yeah, your connect's been robbing you guys blind. Been stretching the product."

Damn. All this time I noticed fiends had been coming to me complaining about their high. I even drew my fire on a couple of those who got in my face. They had good reason to be angry. The dope wasn't coming back. When coke goes out, it's supposed to drop. We were already not getting a lion's share of the profits although we took the most risks. Now I found out that black fiends weren't even valued enough to be served quality coke.

Life is ironic though. If I didn't go to jail that day, I'd probably have been dead that night. The package was to be delivered to one of Miami's other dope kingpins, who didn't take kindly to being ripped off. God works in mysterious ways I guess. I couldn't see it back then to understand this divine intervention during the worst of times. I was staring down my future with a handful of rotten eggs.

I still didn't give up any names. That wasn't part of the rules of engagement. It was against the G code. It might sound crazy to the civilized world, but a person will never understand if he or she hasn't walked that road. My crew had families. They supported younger brothers and sisters. I couldn't jeapordize their well-being because I got caught up in some shit. Each world has its principles. I made this bed, now I had to sleep in it. Even if it was laid out next to those I chose to avoid in this life for my own sanity.

The cops gave up. "It's your ass, kid. Sleep tight in the pen."

The lawyer sauntered in after they left. He checked my temperature. "How we holding up?"

"I'm cool," I answered.

"Seriously, how are we holding up?" This time he peered into me. He dug deep into my core. In that moment, my life hung in the balance. Every decision one makes definitely has consequences.

"Look, y'all ain't got to worry about me. Just leave my family out the shit," I said.

He was out of there faster than I could say 'bye. Just like that, my time had run its course. Some other young, hopeless kid would push their product. Finding new workers was easy given the other economic options in Miami.

My family completely washed their hands of me. I had brought too much drama to everyone. I knew I hit rock bottom because folks reached the point at which they were tired of my very sight, like a rash that won't go away. My presence caused a bad taste in everyone's mouth. I was the pariah. I was permanently put out the house. I stayed with Tronne the weeks before my sentencing. His mother, who we called Ms. Fish, was always good to me. She always took me in when I got kicked out. Even when she was advised otherwise, she took me in. I could see where Tronne got it from. His mother had a heart of gold.

My rap sheet already reflected I was a career criminal.

Society could have done better without the likes of me. At that moment I realized why some guys killed themselves. It's so easy to throw in the towel.

At the arraignment the judge's tone was much the same: "Once again you're in my courtroom. Time and time again you've been given chances, but you're determined to continue down this reckless path." He looked at my public defender. "Not surprising that no guardian has showed for your defendant. I would be fed up too."

I pleaded guilty. It was the best option I had. The judge threw the book at me. He tried me as an adult. I was sentenced to four years in prison for armed trafficking with intent to distribute cocaine. I was only sixteen.

I spent the next several weeks trying to get my weight up, so to speak. Anyone in the juvenile detention center who tried me, I dealt with. I heard stories from the older hustlers who revolved in and out the pen when they came home. They advised on making sure one's reputation was trunk tight before going inside. Guys in my hood would do a bid like they went on vacation. The same way suburban kids are destined for college, prison was inevitable for us.

My transfer out of the detention center took longer than expected, but I got ready that morning and prepared for the worst. This was the final stop. I wasn't dead, so prison was the next best thing. I had a cast on from a broken arm I had suffered in a fight. I was handicapped already.

Anyone who says he wasn't scared when he went to prison for the first time at my age is a damn liar. I was terrified. Smacking around and firing on a couple rivals on the strip was one thing. Going into a zoo overrun by the men society keeps far away from civilized folks is another. No one inmate is the most dangerous inmate in the pen. One guy in there will garner the most respect, but you better believe every minute he's in there he's being tested. If there was a hell, it couldn't be worse than where I was headed. If there was such a place, it would prove my fear at the time that fate truly loves some and not others.

30

Rain It Pours

THEY CALLED IT THE TENTH FLOOR AND I ARRIVED there on my seventeenth birthday. The Tenth Floor of the Miami-Dade County jail housed the most violent and hardened felons. It was our house of pain. It took what seemed like an hour for my transfer to clear, but the first thing I learned about prison was that my time was not mine. My life wasn't mine either. I was state property. Dressed in my orange jumpsuit, I went to be processed. The corrections officer had me pick out the items from my box that I was allowed to take with me. They told me to get stamps, phone numbers, one picture, and one of everything for hygiene, such as deodorant. I had to place everything else on the table. They gave me the choice to donate the extra stuff or take it home in thirty days.

Those guards knew no one was going home in thirty days. One inmate that was sentenced to thirty years had arrived the same day as me. He was caught trying to sneak something else out of his box. The guy was huge. He was one of those husky country brothers probably raised on fresh milk and hogs' feet. He was the Humpty Dumpty of the cellblock. Those guards made his fat ass sing happy birthday to me all the way to my bunk. It was humiliating for us both.

Welcome to prison, nigga.

If you think those beat cops hate their lives more than any other government employee, think again. Those COs were the worst. A person couldn't meet a more sadistic breed than the men and women society pays to guard its prisoners. Something about those walls chipped away at everyone's humanity after a while. They hated their jobs, but they hated us more. I thought since neither of us wanted to be there, they would make the time as bearable as possible. *Look, asshole, I don't like coming to this piss-and-shit-infested crap shoot, staring at you sorry inmates. But if we gotta be in here, let's make the best of it. You let me pass the time watching* Sanford and Son *reruns and I'll let you go beat your dick off in peace.*

That was too civilized for prison life. They made us the punching bag for every regret suffered in their lives. Imagine an open wound being stabbed with a nail constantly. That day the mind games began. I shook my head.

"Oh, you don't like that, little nigga? What the fuck you gonna do about it? Try that stone-cold shit in here and I'll gut you," said the CO. "I'll body you, nigga."

I felt like choking that guard, but something told me otherwise. I got the sense that he was dead serious. It seemed he would be happy to break my neck. The world I was engulfed in right now looked insane. The faces staring outside those bars looked cold to me. As I walked by, I could tell there was no peace here. In a moment of optimism I thought maybe I'd get the stability that was missing in my life in the pen. It sounded good at least. But this place was crazier than all the madness out on Fifteenth Avenue.

"Trustee! Trustee!" one inmate hollered for the inmate assigned to run errands. "My toilet's backed up! The shit stinks in here!"

The trustee was usually the best-behaved inmate. He wasn't a snitch or the CO's pet or anything like that. He was the guy in there that got along with everybody. He was the person who made the place a bit more hospitable with a kind word or two. The COs gave him a bit more breathing room than the other inmates. In return he served as a broker between us and them. That day the CO wasn't in a good mood so the trustee couldn't help.

"What you hollering about?" the CO asked.

"Ain't got no water coming to my cell," said the inmate. "The toilet's been clogged since yesterday."

"Do I look like a plumber, nigga!" yelled the CO. "This shit ain't the Holiday Inn."

"How am I gonna brush my teeth?"

"Get creative."

Humpty Dumpty offered me some sobering advice. "Look, partner, just keep your head low. Those crackers already got you in a hole, don't dig it no deeper."

He spoke from experience. He had already served time in the chain gang. He was trying to put me up on game. I tried soaking it in, but I felt more like dying. I shuffled past the stares and crazed faces locked in cages. This wasn't like high school where the new kid got the love. The new kid got tested.

"Aight, my nigga, this your spot. Be easy," he told me when we reached the cell.

You can't be serious.

I looked at the large cage with nearly fifty inmates all packed in like a dog pound. Some were laid out on floor mattresses. One guy was curled around a toilet. There were bunk beds, but the place was packed beyond capacity. The crime rate in Miami was so high the jail was overcrowded. The Tenth Floor looked more like a homeless shelter. I walked over to the bunk that was assigned to me, but before I could put my stuff on the bed, someone stopped me.

"Hold up, my nigga, that's my bed," said Lil Bo, creeping up behind me. He wasn't more than five feet tall, but judging from his scowl, Lil Bo seemed to be a force to be reckoned with. I had seen him around my way in the hood before.

"What nigga?" said Lil Bo, trying to bait me into a confrontation. I hadn't been on the Tenth Floor more than a day and already this guy wanted me to bring the heat. I put my stuff down. He clenched his fist. The other inmates in the room stood up. The wagering began.

"I got two cigarettes on buddy with the cash!"

One inmate offered me his mat. I turned to look at the CO, but he was placing a bet on Lil Bo to whup my ass. The thought of choking this dude to death brought a particular happiness. Fuck the repercussions. I wanted to break Lil Bo's neck for trying me. Then, suddenly, he backed off. The crowd scattered like roaches when the closet light is turned on. A familiar voice from outside the cell quelled my inner storm.

"Me and Shrimp gotta bunk for you over here bruh."

Big Black was standing at the entrance. I paused. I can't explain how I felt when I saw Black. Before I could speak, Black had the inmate who'd offered me his mat hemmed up on the wall.

"Ain't nothing sweet round here, motherfucker!" he yelled at the dude.

Black wasn't overreacting. In the pen, newcomers who sit on another inmate's bed get their shit pushed in. There were inmates in there trying to make a young inmate his baby. At night while we slept, the baby would serve his daddy his snacks, if you know what I mean. No one who isn't family to you before you go to prison offers you anything for *free*.

"You're cool? I see you're still outta control," said Black, pointing to the cast on my arm.

He took me over to his spot in the cage. Black commanded everyone's respect. It wasn't because he was a bully. He was an honorable dude. Even those seen as unlawful and ungodly to larger society follow a code of ethics. People respect integrity. Black was all of the above. Word had already got to him that I was on my way in, so he had reserved a bed for me under his.

Black had the top bunk in the corner. It's what in prison we called the throne. The vents from the AC were located there as well as the television. The cool air and midday game shows weren't the only reasons for wanting that spot. In most cases, it could mean life or death. In a brawl, the bottom bunk left an inmate vulnerable for an enemy to dive in and shank him. The top gave one a vantage point.

"I gotta see everything that's going down," said Black.

In an open-space dorm with lots of beds, the slimiest dude

in a crew would sleep somewhere off in the middle so he could be away from the drama when it popped off. When I got over to Black's area, it was more like a family reunion.

Shrimp, Lil Wil, Lil Al, Melvin, Puerto Ric, and Carmelio were there. They were some of the coldest cats I knew in the street. All had carried a considerable amount of weight. So I started to feel like I was gaining my footing in what was to become my new home. We talked about the snitches and weak cats who folded in the interrogation room. That I held my own in that room earned me respect from the crew, but the brief moment without drama was of course interrupted.

"Partna, I'm gonna deal with you! You could put my old girl on that!" Lil Bo yelled across the hall.

I wasn't having it. This guy was asking for the pain and I wanted to bring it. I turned to Carmelio. "Bruh, take my cast off."

Black and the crew look dumbfounded. They knew I had heart, but now I was ready to brawl with one arm.

"Bruh, if you can't take it off, just hold my arm down for me," I said. Everyone shook their heads. Then the hall erupted in laughter. Even Lil Bo was chuckling.

"We just wanted to see if you were gonna fight, bruh," he told me, turning to Big Black.

"You still the truth, bruh," Black said.

I should have known all along they were just testing my temperature. Black carried the most weight in there. He didn't want to cosign a chump. He was headed for a life bid after he left the county. I was just passing through. I know he would have looked out for me regardless. He was that type of guy, but knowing that I could hold my own made it a bit less tiresome to watch over me in this madhouse. That night I tried to sleep. I tried to doze off and think about my plan to stay sane while I did my time, but the screams across the hall woke me.

The inmate I saw curled up around the toilet was getting the life beat out of him. The word on the floor was that he came in a couple hours before me. He was all messed up when they escorted him to the cell, crying and begging to go home. The rules on the street apply in prison. Weakness is a death sentence. One inmate was pissing on his head, while another was taking a dump. The CO walked by laughing.

"You cool, bruh?" Black asked me. "You look like you all deep in thought and shit."

"I'm cool, Black. Just gotta lot of shit on my mind."

"Well, don't think too much. That's how cats end up going off the deep end in here."

31

Amerika

It's safe to say that Florida's prisons are among the most dangerous and hostile in America. The other candidates for the penitentiary horror awards are Texas and California. I've never been in a Cali or Texan prison so I'll stick with Florida.

It took Jesse Tafero getting his head burned off for the powers that be to finally consider getting rid of Old Sparky. That's the pet name U.S. prison officials gave the electric chair. The first time it was used in Florida was in 1890. They had been cooking inmates in that thing for more than a century. Even crazy old Ted Bundy was roasted in it. It claimed the lives of exactly 217 inmates.

On May 4, 1990, the chair's penchant for shooting fireworks

got put on display in Starke. I'm sure it wasn't the first time prison officials saw the explosion that was about to take place. They probably ate popcorn during the show.

Tafero wasn't a choirboy by any means, but nobody deserves to go out like that. He was sentenced to death for killing a cop. After they turned the chair on, Tafero's head caught on fire. The officials watched him roast for about four minutes before they pulled the chord. Florida's attorney general, Robert Butterworth, even said the chair's fiery rep would prevent violent crime. Protesters took to the streets. Florida banned the chair for the next six years, but somehow they got it back frying again, until two similar incidents permanently eliminated it in 2002.

After the Tafero jailhouse barbecue, another death-row inmate became the center of a media firestorm over abuse at Florida prisons. Frank Valdes was sentenced to die after allegedly killing a corrections officer in 1987. He started writing letters about the harsh conditions in Florida State Prison. Then in 1999 he was beaten to death by three guards. During the investigation of the incident, Warden James Crosby warned employees at the prison to "quit acting like a bunch of criminals" because many weren't cooperating with authorities. Although Crosby had come under fire for the negligence at the prison that led to the incident, Governor Jeb Bush put the guy in charge of the entire Florida Department of Corrections in 2003.

That same year, seventeen-year-old Omar Paisley died at the same Miami-Dade Juvenile Detention Center where I was locked up before going to prison. Nurses ignored his constant pleas for help after his appendix burst. Even more shocking than Paisely's death was the brutal beating of fourteen-year-old Martin Lee Anderson, caught on video at a Panama City boot camp in 2006. The video shows the guards beating and kicking the young brother, but the autopsy report they filed stated he died from sickle-cell anemia. An investigation later proved he died of suffocation. However, the seven guards and one nurse charged with manslaughter of a child were acquitted. Then the big kahuna himself took a fall later that same year.

James Crosby pled guilty to bribery charges. He was running a prison mafia of sorts. Guards had admitted to smuggling in drugs, women, and all sorts of shit. Guards who didn't comply with the order of the land got beat down. Crosby was sentenced to eight years at FCI Morgantown in West Virginia. Authorities were wise not to put him in a Florida prison. Those previously mentioned were put in charge of me and the other ninety thousand inmates in Florida prisons. They were supposed to keep order and civility before we were released back to the neighborhood. So try to figure out how more messed up we became. Our masters were crooks masked behind a badge.

I had been on the Tenth Floor for a couple months and my transfer to Indian River was coming up. It would be my first trip north of Fort Lauderdale. I should have been getting myself prepared mentally for that long trip, but I was busy raising hell in the county. I was rolling with a serious crew so I had to prove myself. The brawls usually went down in the cafeteria. If I saw an inmate who'd tried me the previous night, I challenged him. My reasoning could have been something as simple as his bumping into me in the cafeteria line. I'd walk right up to him:

"You gotta problem, bruh?"

Slam. I'd hit him in the face with my tray. Then I choked the living hell out of him. I'd try to stomp his head into the floor before the guards came and hauled me off.

"My name's Trick, motherfucker!"

I wanted rivals to *hear* me. I didn't plan on spending my prison years as somebody's bitch. In the pen, violence was necessary. I couldn't run from a man trying to drive a shank in my neck. A guard with a grudge was on the other side of the cell.

The only break I took from fighting was phoning home on the weekend. Tater stayed home so he could accept my calls. He usually rounded up a couple of my girlfriends for me, but I was more interested in what was happening on the block. It was the same old same old. My crew was trying to maintain, but the life was definitely catching up to us.

Soon after I got jammed, Dante caught a drug charge. He was sentenced to two years at Brevard in Cocoa. I was determined to get back out there as soon as I finished my bid. However, my frequent fights on the Tenth Floor weren't helping to speed up my release.

When the time finally came for me to leave for Indian River, the guards and other inmates were well aware of my reputation. The camp sat up in Vero Beach. It's funny how a lot of Florida's prisons sit a stone's throw away from retirees and vacation spots. When I got there, I was surprised at the respect inmates showed me. The place wasn't as bad as the Tenth Floor. It housed inmates from ages fourteen to eighteen of all classifications. I started taking classes to get my GED and even picked up a trade. I had always been pretty crafty outside from my days raking grass so I took up landscaping. It got my mind off those prison bars for the time being.

My release was right around the corner when my roommate got me hauled to the box. Inmates actually go to jail in jail. That's what the box is. My roommate knew I had a side hustle besides going to my GED and landscaping classes. I sold sweets: cookies, chocolate bars, wafers. The sugary treats you pass in the grocery store are like diamonds to a man locked down. We used to sneak in boxes upon boxes of the stuff. At Indian River I was a one-stop shop for the goodies. I used the proceeds to gamble. Toonk was our favorite card game. On the evening I got sent to the hole, I was playing toonk with another inmate before he accused me of cheating. I wasn't having it. We began fighting. I'm sure he knew I wasn't cheating. He probably just wanted to vent some frustration. Guys on the inside were live wires ready to explode at any minute. My roommate never paid attention to any fights on the hall, but this time he intervened. He called the guard to break it up. We were sent downstairs while the guard searched the cell. When I came back, I opened the hole in the wall where I kept the money I won from gambling. It wasn't there.

My roommate had been eyeing my piggy bank for months. He waited until I stacked enough bread before he found a reason to steal it. He showed the guard the boxes of strawberry cream cookies I had hidden. The guard and I struck a deal. If I ate the hundreds of cookies within a half hour, I wouldn't have the incident added to my record. Soon, the whole prison was a sea of cookies. I was literally shitting pink. Trouble just lengthened my stay and messed up my parole chances. I had to keep my head low so I could finally get the hell out of there. I did.

32

Thug Life Again

I DON'T REMEMBER THE MORNING I WAS RELEASED A year later, but I can still feel the breeze and smell the fresh air. An inmate never thinks he'll actually leave prison. Imagine the steel door closing behind you. In that moment the noises, stench, and cold stares are whisked away by freedom breeze. Just like that, you're on the other side of that wall. You tell yourself you're never going back to that hell. It all seems like a bad dream that you just woke from. In reality it was a bad dream that lasted one year. I was dressed in a black Nike windbreaker jumpsuit with matching hot-pink-and-black sneakers that Hollywood bought me. I looked around. Wood was sitting in his Benz, waving me over. His right-hand man, Fatso, was parked behind in Wood's Nissan Maxima.

"Back home, bruh! You cool?" Wood asked.

"Yeah, I'm straight, bruh. I tell you this much. That shit ain't the place to be."

Wood gazed at me. He didn't have to say it. I knew he was proud of me. I didn't make any excuses for my fall. I took it in stride. He always wanted better for me. He thought I was the one that could actually make it out without being a slave to the powder. He believed in me when I didn't. We cruised the strip. It was the same old shit out there. Fiends were on the corners and the dope boys served them. I wasn't sure if it was time for me to make that left at the crossroads or just get back on the corner.

We pulled up to Wood's mother's house. My house was still off-limits. I wasn't surprised that no one threw some welcome-home party for me. That stuff only happens in the movies. I laugh when I see those scenes.

Most guys I was locked up with had nowhere to go upon release. They most likely ended up at a halfway house or homeless shelter. In many cases their girlfriend had already run off with the partner the ex-con broke bread with in the street. His family had moved on. Some dudes couldn't be released until they confirmed an address to be released to. Considering that reality, I was lucky that I still had Wood.

After hanging out for some time, he asked me to go pick Keba up from school. I took the Maxima and headed out. When I'd dropped her off, there was a brawl outside the school. Things definitely hadn't changed. Later that day I ran into one of Wood's friends who was showing off his newest BMW convertible. It was cold as ice. I wanted to take it for a spin. It had been a while since I was behind the wheel of such a dope ride.

"Damn, bruh. Let me hold the 'vert for a minute," I told him.

He obliged. I picked up a couple of my friends and cruised the strip. We were high-rolling for the minute. Then one of my friends jumped out and raced toward a kid he had been beefing with. A fight ensued.

Damn, here we go again.

Trouble followed me everywhere. I couldn't shake her. I contemplated telling him to calm down because my friend was getting the best of the kid, whose uncle had now popped the trunk of his car. I thought he was reaching for a gun so I grabbed the pistol I had under the seat and unloaded. I fired a couple shots in the air to defuse the situation.

My friend jumped in and we sped off, but the kid's uncle wasn't finished. He came to Wood's house later that day and confronted me.

"Oh, you think you're a man! All right, we'll see. I'ma treat you like a man!" he yelled.

I thought I was going to have to kill him, but he left. The next two months I just drifted. I was trying to find myself, but something strange was happening when I went to visit my probation officer. She was never there.

I was soon called into a mandatory probation hearing. Before I could even enter the room, the officer was in there burying me to the judge:

"Your Honor, he's never showed up to my office, and he doesn't comply with any of the requirements. He also failed his urine test."

I tried to defend myself. "Your Honor, how can I fail a urine test if she says she's never seen me?"

Then the district attorney dropped the bombshell. "He's also been charged with attempted murder," she said.

I couldn't believe it. The kid's uncle who came by to confront me had pressed charges that same day and I didn't know it. The judge looked at me like I was crazy. I couldn't blame him. I had only myself to blame. Who the hell violates their probation a couple hours after they're released? I wish I had the good sense back then to use my mistakes as a tool to keep my anger in check. I didn't.

I was sentenced to two and a half more years. This time around I was scarred and I didn't give a damn. This was the last stop. I was now a twice-convicted felon, and the place I was headed made Indian River look like summer camp. The longest sentences served there was around nine years. At my new home to be, many of the inmates were serving life sentences. Picture a thousand condemned men all hemmed inside rotting walls, bursting at the seams. In state prison the older inmates with the longest sentences never caused the most trouble. The younger ones with the shortest sentences, who had the most to lose, caused all the mayhem. They usually got messed up by the ones with all the time who had nothing to lose. I was that young hothead.

33

N-word

THE BUS RIDE THAT AUGUST DAY IN 1992, TO Apalachee Correctional Institution West, was the longest of my life. With Hurricane Andrew soon approaching, prison officials wanted to get us processed as soon as possible. It gave me hours to reflect on where I had been, but I had no clue where I was going. I was sure I'd be just another sorry brother forever locked in the chain gang. The prison was in Sneads.

This wasteland of a town had a population of about one thousand. The prison was the town's main attraction of sorts. Prisons usually generate the most revenue for the town the prison is located in. Sneads sat twenty-five miles from the Alabama border. I was officially in the Deep South. The horror stories of the racial tensions in those towns where Alabama meets

Florida are well documented. I would have to get used to being called a nigger by redneck COs. Some donned tattoos of black babies hung by nooses.

The living quarters were similar to those of the Tenth Floor; we were packed in one large room with bunk beds scattered throughout. At Apalachee the bloodshed was horrific. Inmates simply walked up to foes and shanked them.

I didn't carry many weapons during my last bid. It wasn't necessary. In here I had to adapt. Inmates got creative with the tools they made to cut rivals. We carved toothbrushes into shanks, others were molded from melted plastic. Fights usually went down in the yard. One inmate would just run up behind another one and cut him. It wasn't out of the ordinary to see an inmate running across the yard with blood streaking down his neck. At night the screams kept me awake. I'd wake up to an inmate lying on the floor, coughing up his life. The place was a nightmare.

But once again God sent me a guide. I hadn't listened to Booner and Junior when they tried. Fudge did his best. It seemed the only person that could reach me at this point was someone I thought was more street-certified. It had to be somebody who I thought I couldn't beat down, someone I respected.

His name was Papa Stick. He was seventy-eight years old, the oldest in Apalachee and the oldest inmate I've ever met. When I first got to Apalachee, I was upset that they put me in the cot next to his. I didn't want to spend my time next to a guy that could have been my grandfather. At night, Stick mumbled some mumbo jumbo while he read one of the hundred books he always kept. I wanted to holler at him to shut his trap, but something told me otherwise.

Although he hobbled around the prison, no one disrespected Stick. During lunch, inmates served him extra food. He was given extended library visits. Most of us at Apalachee could have been his grandsons. Oddly enough, Stick was in prison for killing a twelve-year-old boy. I didn't know the particulars of the case, but I knew he wished he could take it back. He was an old-timer from Tampa. I noticed something else about Stick. I was the only inmate he conversed with. Well, not exactly conversed.

"An eagle lost among crows gets stuck in the cornfields," he would tell me. Stick spoke in riddles. It was up to you to figure out the point he was making. "I can't be bothered with these jitterbugs. If you like being stuck in a dog's butt hole, go run with the fleas, just don't bring the itching round me."

At night, our conversations took my mind off the inmate across the room getting stabbed to death. Battles from the yard carried over far into the wee hours of the morning. The lower bunk left one vulnerable, but my stay on the Tenth Floor had me prepared. Inmates waited for rivals to go to sleep, then swooped in with a vengeance. I half slept most nights with my shank tucked underneath me.

Stick always shook his head at the mayhem. No one crossed him though.

"The inmates all respect you," I told him.

"They respect you too," he replied.

I began to see what he was trying to tell me. I was different from the other inmates. I could read and write really well. He lent me a lot of his books to read. I was pretty good at math also. Stick saw the light in me when I didn't. Prison time forces a man to read between the lines. Other inmates studied me hard. No one understands human nature more than a convicted felon; not even a Harvard degree educates more about the inner workings of the human mind than prison halls.

Patience is a virtue learned in prison. In most cases one's sanity and life depend on it. In the game of life, most times success depends on it. In the boardroom, a rash decision can cost big money. In prison it can cost your life.

When every minute of every day is spent trying to survive in a pound filled with condemned men, one learns to observe their habits. I learned what made other inmates tick. I listened more than I talked. I couldn't survive my prison sentence without patience. Patience was my best friend. She was better to me than any lover could have been. I finally cracked Stick's riddles. He had the rest of his life to mull over the past. He was going to die in prison. He tried to show me that my life was far from over. All I had to do was keep my head low and, like the cliché goes, "do the time and don't let the time do me." I could either live day by day and inch toward my freedom or race through in a rage-fueled, blood-soaked mania. I chose the latter.

"I didn't know jitterbugs could read," Stick would tell me. "Well, those crackers could always use another coon."

Stick's words hit me in the chest even if they were veiled in codes. Straight talk would only have put an already wounded young man on the defensive. If I was so special, why did God leave me stuck in here?

Oh, well. I began running with the crew from Dade, Broward, and Palm Beach counties. We fought the inmates from Tampa and St. Petersburg. Although we were all from Florida, we divided ourselves along geographic lines and were determined to gut each other before our bids were up. The feuding got so bad that on one occasion we started a full-scale riot.

Guards blamed me and a couple others for starting it and sent me to the box.

After my time in the box was up, the folks at Apalachee cut me loose. They labeled me a danger to the facility and had me transferred. I didn't mind because my days were filled with misery at that place. I boarded the bus for Okaloosa Correctional Institution in Crestview. Wars carried over from prison to prison, so some inmates in there were waiting to cut me up for stabbing their friends at Apalachee. At Okaloosa the guards seemed more preoccupied with causing trouble than the inmates themselves.

The night I got there I was lined up with the other transfers, shackled from head to toe, getting ready to be transported to my cell. I guess we looked like a bunch of Sambos because that's what the guards started chanting as we walked to our cells. They taunted us for more than five minutes before the other inmates started banging their cell doors. The place erupted. Inmates threw toilet paper and overturned their mattresses. The guards were outnumbered. We took over the prison. The alarms went off. Then the riot squad rushed in and pepper-sprayed us all. Some inmates got tasered. Lockdown.

I was once again blamed for the melee and processed for transfer. I soon boarded a bus headed to Baker in Sanderson. My reputation throughout the state's penitentiary system grew with every fight. Word on the cellblocks was that the inmate Trick had a screw loose. I didn't take any particular value in the disposition. It just seemed like my whole life someone had to try me. I could be in the park and the damn resident wino would even test me. It's like I had a sign on my my forehead that screamed DRAMA, I'M OVER HERE!

I found myself spending most of my time at Baker in the box. One night the brilliant powers that be decided to put an emergency transfer in there with me. I'm not sure if it was intentional or not, but the guards put my life at risk. Emergency transfers are inmates who are deemed mentally unstable and unfit to be with other prisoners. In other words, they're insane. They have to be evaluated before being placed into the general population.

This inmate was cuckoo. He didn't realize he was in prison or believe he should be in prison. I woke in the wee hours of the morning with this nut case staring down on me.

"Who you, nigga?" he asked.

This was just my luck. I was locked away with a lunatic. I didn't think it was possible to have bad luck in prison. It's where I ended up because I was at the bottom of my luck already.

"You're from Miami, huh?"

Oh, boy. I knew what that meant. Hustlers from Miami had a reputation for making a lot of money. Miami dope boys had the cars and women; the combination birthed envy. It made us targets. The yelling ensued:

"I can't stand you Miami motherfuckers! Y'all think y'all run shit! I'll show you who run shit, motherfucker!"

He punched me square in the jaw. We began fighting. I thought the guards would let us maul each other to death down there, but they came running down the hall. They knew they could get into deep trouble because there had been recent outcries in the media about poor treatment of mentally ill inmates at Florida prisons. This is one time I was grateful for those academic types that visited the prisons.

When the guards finally had him handcuffed, I began

whaling on him. There's no such thing as a fair fight. Don't believe the hype. In the melee I busted my head wide-open on the toilet and was sent to the infirmary. As a consolation prize for their mistake, prison officials let me choose the prison I wanted to be transferred to after my confinement. I chose Desoto.

34

Thug Holiday

DESOTO WAS *THE* PLACE TO BE FOR FELONS IN FLOR-
ida. Back then, Desoto was the Madison Square Garden of prisons. A bunk at Desoto was like making it to the major leagues.
The prison was close enough to Miami to know what went on
in the streets. Family members could make the short trip for
visits.

For me it ended up being a homecoming of sorts. Black,
Tronne, Melvin, and my older brother Cedric met me at check-
in. Cedric had the same DNA that Hollywood and I had inher-
ited. Our veins pumped a hustler's blood. More than half my
brothers have served time in prison. Cedric got jammed on a
drug-trafficking charge. He was considered one of the older hustlers in the streets. I was happy to see those guys. I didn't get to

spend much time with Ced growing up. We ran into each other on the streets, but he was making his money and I was making mine. Tronne was locked up for armed robbery. Prison forced a much needed reunion party.

That's how prison goes. My life and that of the brothers' I shared space with amid those walls forever intertwined. We bumped into each other along the way and formed lifelong bonds. There's no room for pride when someone's forced to use a toilet a yard away from another man. Prison is the truest fraternity. We didn't share pledges and Greek letters. We shared life and death.

On many occasions I would have died in there if not for Black, Ced, Tronne, or another one from my crew. Guards would have found me in a cell with my guts ripped open. I depended on my band of brothers. We shared commissary and everything else. At Desoto we ran the yard. Black, Melvin, and Ced had already earned their stripes. I still got into fights nevertheless. I was too volatile. The slightest cold stare or mean glance sent me upside someone's head. I spent more time in confinement than I did on the yard. I used to spend 180 days at a time in the box. We were bored out of our minds down there. Breakfast came in at 4 a.m. Lunch was served at 10:30 a.m., then dinner at 3 p.m. We were left starving with nothing to do for hours. We got creative to pass the time. One inmate could sing. Another inmate pretended to be a human beat box, and one inmate quoted Bible scriptures.

Each person was given his time of silence to perform. We couldn't see each other, but we could hear each other. The only thing that interrupted that moment was a flushed toilet. I remember a couple of inmates whose throats were slit over flushing the potty. That time in confinement was the most sacred moment for any convicted felon, if there was such a thing in prison. We called it riding the bars.

When it was my turn, everyone took extra notice. In fact, inmates started giving up their time to me. I rapped. My verses were laced with the real-life pain we suffered through. I rhymed about the friends I saw die in the streets. Their blood-soaked corpses evoked memories.

A couple months before, word had reached me that my childhood friend Darryl had been shot to death. He was set up by his right-hand man, who told Darryl's supplier that Darryl was ripping him off. It wasn't true, but in the dope game someone always tried to knock a friend out the way to get to the top. My other playground friend O'Sean suffered a similar fate, but ended up paralyzed before he passed away. The bullet inched its way to his heart over time. As the news came in about my deceased comrades, it gave me more material to rap about. I couldn't cry. Rapping was the best way to express my pain.

"Trick, my homeboy used my baby mama to set me up!" one inmate would yell from his cell. "Can you lace something for me, bruh?"

My rhymes became prison therapy. I was narrating our lives. Soon word spread throughout the cellblock that the wild inmate Trick had a way with words. Black brought inmates who wanted me to pen love letters to folks back home. Others asked me to write appeal letters. I started rapping in the yard and on the cellblock. Even the guards gathered around to hear me spit. When anyone from my crew phoned home, they held the phone in the direction of where I was rapping. I had become an in-house MC.

"Bruh, you should start writing down your raps," Black told me. Ced agreed. It was the only thing besides busting heads that came natural to me, so I gave it a shot. Before long, we were sending my songs to Hollywood. He began promoting events and was planning on getting a record label off the ground with his partner, Ted. Their group, Nu Vibes, wasn't making any waves. Wood still wanted me to be the face of the label.

Ted, though, wasn't sure I was a wise investment. My track record showed that all I seemed to be dedicated to was landing in prison. It was a hard pill to swallow. Long ago I had given up on myself, so I couldn't expect people to jump on my bandwagon. That wagon always seemed to be leaning off a cliff. I was determined nonetheless and kept writing. I had finally found something to hold on to. I always decided to be the best at what I set out to do. If I was going to be a rapper, I planned to be the coldest emcee. Things were looking up for me. Then the night of June 22, 1994, swept in like a hurricane.

35

Thugs Don't Live Long

It was pouring rain that day. Passing showers are customary during Miami summers. The sun emerges after about fifteen minutes of thundering, but that day the rain didn't stop. I'll never forget how violently the sky roared that night. I was boxing with someone from the crew. The sparring kept us in shape. My name blared over the in-house intercom. I was being called into the main office, then I caught a glimpse of Ced racing across the yard toward me. He nearly ran over everyone in the cafeteria as he made his way toward me.

"Watch out, bruh!"

Inmates were yelling at Ced to be careful, but he kept on running like a bat out of hell. I made my way down the stairs to meet him. When our eyes connected, I *knew*. He didn't have to utter a word. Things were getting crazy in the streets. The younger hustlers out there weren't respecting the game like back in the day. Dudes were straight setting each other up. Bodies were left cold and crumpled all over the Beans. Things were crazier than when I'd been out there trapping. The chain of events gave me the intuition to understand that Ced was about to confirm my deepest fear. In prison we got the news of anything happening in the streets before the cops made it to the scene. We even knew what was about to happen before it popped off. Incidents that occurred in prison often trickled out into the streets. By now Black and the rest of the crew were gathered at the top of the stairs.

Ced paused to catch his breath. "You wouldn't believe what happened, bruh," he said.

"Wood," I replied.

Ced nodded.

I can't explain the anguish that took over me. Imagine breathing without a heartbeat. Picture standing without legs. Then you fall down inside. The world around you ends. Every feeling at your core turns cold. You're left empty inside.

I didn't want to believe Hollywood was gone. Those who've lost a loved one can relate. Denial offers a bit of momentary peace, but then the horror sinks in. Wood wasn't coming back. They say the hardest men aren't supposed to cry. I cried so much that night even the guards felt sorry for me. Black tried consoling me.

Hollywood's rep made him a target. He had everything every dope boy wanted, but he was the type to give you the shirt off his back. Violence was his last resort. Someone wanted to take the king off his throne. Word on the street was that

Hollywood and his right-hand man, Fatso, got ambushed. Three rivals armed with AR-15 assault rifles converged on them while they were parked at the corner of Northwest Twenty-fifth Avenue and 152nd Street. The attackers emptied more than fifty rounds through the windshield. I don't even know if my brother had time to pull his gun. I still wish I was there. I'd probably have died alongside my brother. It would have been the best way to go.

I stood there as pain consumed me. It subsided to anger. Then I was overcome with rage. I grabbed the shank I kept in the grooves under the toilet and searched for anyone I thought might have had a hand in Wood's death, but the fighting didn't ease my pain. It didn't make sense. Cutting somebody wasn't going to bring Hollywood back. He was gone. All I could do was go to the chaplain to get permission to attend Wood's funeral. I asked to be able to attend with some dignity, but the warden wasn't having it. I arrived at Wood's funeral dressed in my jailhouse suit shackled from head to toe. The large crowd that gathered showed just how much Hollywood was loved. They tried hard not to stare at his shackled younger brother. Miami had lost a prince.

I sat next to Ted. I looked at my brother's corpse in that coffin and realized that I had to make a change. This mess I called my life wasn't cutting it. Rap was going to be my best shot out. I would have to make it so.

I turned to Ted. "Bruh, I'm gonna be on the straight and narrow. I'm not going back to prison when I get out."

It didn't matter if Ted believed me. I wanted out of the madness that just stole my heart. I wanted the world to see who Hollywood was. He could live through my rhymes. I wanted the world to see how we lived in the streets of Miami. If I offered folks a lens to see what we were dealing with, then maybe things could change. My dream was to become a street journalist. I knew rap could give me that opportunity.

Tupac Shakur was doing it. Everyone on the cellblocks was really feeling that cat. His music had a message. He was taking the ghetto's pain to the mainstream. Over in Houston the rapper Scarface was doing much the same thing. They were both emcees whose blueprint a brother like me, going from the pen to the mike, could use as a guide in the fog.

I began writing as soon as I got back to my cell. The lyrics that spilled out on the page were the things that weighed heavy on my heart. I didn't edit or rewrite anything. I was pouring out my soul. In addition to Hollywood, I had already lost five of my closest homeboys while locked up. So it was evident that brothers in the streets didn't live long. I began to write:

> *Now picture me as a killer*
> *Young black dope dealer I'm doing this one for my niggas*
> *Who ride for this*
> *Who even lost they life for this*
> *And them niggas who survivin this*
> *They don't live that long*

Those are lyrics from the song "They Don't Live That Long." Titles came later. I wrote what I was feeling at the time. Most times I was venting.

By the time I finished, I had written about four hundred songs. I mailed the notebook to Ted so he could know I was serious. I spent the rest of my days at Desoto focused on rapping. I promised the inmates in Desoto that I'd take our stories to the mainstream. They believed in me. Life is ironic. I had sought all my life to find somewhere I belonged. Love had eluded me all these years. I found it in those prison walls, among brothers I'd have died for.

"Let the young homeys know this isn't the place, bruh," Black would say. "They don't gotta take this fall."

36

Rags to Riches

I HAD NOTHING WHEN I WAS RELEASED ON JANUARY 25, 1995. I looked around and was alone. The state had taken two and a half years of my life. Wood wasn't there to pick me up. I caught the bus and headed to the Beans. The corners were worse than I had imagined. Liberty City was on fire. The corners mirrored a scene from a Wild West cowboy movie.

My homeboy Big C and his former right-hand man, Tiny, were at war. They had taken over the streets together when the older hustlers went down. Liberty City belonged to Big C's Zombie Squad. They had to cosign anything going down in the neighborhood, but Tiny started robbing the crew. He dressed up in a disguise and robbed his own crew's dope hole.

Big C figured out his former partner's ill-hearted scheme and all hell broke loose. They had the Feds all over America on their asses. The FBI labeled Fifteenth Avenue running through the Beans the most dangerous strip in the United States.

I wandered the corners for a while. It was tempting, but I couldn't go back there. My palms sweated, craving to clutch the powder. Even Big C wanted me to take the rap game global. I couldn't get a day job, but I had managed to make a cassette with my songs. I gave it to a couple of homeboys to blast in their rides. Lil Nut was one of the few friends who wasn't dead or locked up yet. He bumped the tape in his car. Everyone thought it was ice-cold. Then I saw a flyer for a talent show Uncle Luke was hosting at the Pac-Jam. The grand prize was a recording contract to become part of the new 2 Live Crew.

I planned to win. No one was going to take what I believed was mines away from me. I even told all my friends I was going to win. They took it with a grain of salt. People were sure I'd be back behind bars within the month. That night, the Pac-Jam was filled to capacity. Everyone showed up. From the Beans all the way down to Homestead, folks wanted to see if the rumors about my skills on the mike were true. I had to deliver.

After the dance group No Good But So Good performed, it was my turn. Most people recount some story of lightning and thunder moving through their bodies during their moment of truth. I didn't experience that grand epiphany. After the shoot-outs, prison riots, and murdered friends, nothing on this planet could have spooked me. Luke played "Captain D's Coming" and I waited. Then I ripped my verse. I didn't even finish the verse before the crowd erupted. People went crazy. Luke nearly had to shut the club down. *Finally.*

I wouldn't say I cried, but the moment was retribution. All my life, I couldn't catch a break. I'm just a skinny kid from the Beans who was trying to find his place in a fucked-up world. That's it. In life most people just need one shot. They just need an opportunity for someone to throw them the rock. The ball always seemed to sail clear over my head. You can't knock a man for turning down the wrong alley if all the other routes have roadblocks.

I closed my eyes.

I'm in the first phase of my dream. Now please don't wake me up. God, let this be a real dream. Everything in my life has been a nightmare. Please let this be real.

Trick Daddy Dollars was born.

The dream was as real as a heart attack. Things happened fast. Luke Records was the first independent label owned by an artist. A lot of folks believe that's why the powers that be gave him so much trouble. As I mentioned earlier, a black man on top is a threat in America, but also some in the community felt he did a disservice to black women with songs like "Me So Horny" and "Pop That Coochie." America hadn't seen women getting down like that in music videos before.

It isn't our fault our women were blessed with curves. All I can say is that Luke gave this brother that opportunity I talked about earlier. Hell, he was the only person I could remember back then really doing anything charitable in the community. His football league gave a lot of kids an alternative besides robbing and dope dealing.

But the censorship battles took their toll on Luke's record label. Someone needed to resurrect the Miami sound in the mainstream. He had signed JT Money and Deboniar, who formed the Poison Clan. They were putting out some dope music. Miami needed to be put back in the forefront. Luke put me on the song "Scarred" and the rest is history. The song was a huge hit and brought Miami back to the forefront of hip-hop. Laying down my verse wasn't much work because I took it from the material I wrote in prison. A year ago I was in a six-by-nine-foot cell. Now, I was rapping my behind off in a music video on MTV. I lived in Luke's condo. The place sure beat a prison cell. I was on my way, but Luke's legal troubles had his label going down in ruins. He had to let go of me and a couple of his other acts like Tre+6 along with several of his employees.

Ted stepped in, his apprehension about signing me having dissipated. Now he knew I was a gold mine, so I became the face of Slip-n-Slide Records. Putting out my first album, *Based on a True Story*, was easy. The title was self-explanatory. Like my verse in "Scarred," most of the songs were written in prison. Many of the records were dedicated to Hollywood. In fact, most of the songs on my first three albums were written in prison. It's why people always tell me they feel the pain in my music. Those lyrics aren't some scripted shit penned in some fancy recording studio. We got a distribution deal from an independent label called Warlock Records and hit the ground running.

I wanted to bring my whole crew with me. This was their moment in the sun as much as it was mines. Dante came straight out of prison to hop in the studio and give us a song he had written in prison called "Killa Head a Body Head." The song's lyrics were some heartfelt gutter shit he was feeling in the cage. We sought out Tronne and Tater, but they were busy making major moves in the street. You could say I took that fork in the road, but we stayed close. Whatever they needed, if I could provide, I did. Ted's plan was for me and another dope emcee named Buddy Roe to come out as a supergroup. Buddy Roe and me were like brothers from another mother musically. We were both raw and soon became connected at the hip. Then he got jammed for cocaine trafficking. That white girl is seductive indeed. Once again I hit a brick wall. Roe and I were like a two-headed monster. We had already laid down tons of tracks. The streets were going to be ours, but I sucked it up for what it was. Roe gave me his blessing to continue making music. In that moment I wanted to throw in the towel. Who was I kidding? Everyone and everything around me was reinforcing the truth.

Trick is just a dope-dealing crook trying his hand at music. Soon enough folks would see the light and he'll be back in the pen like all of his comrades.

God gave me the strength to stay on track when Roe went in. Our street team pushed my records out the trunks of cars, flea markets, and even corner stores. Call it guerrilla marketing. Master P had done it. He showed America the power of the grassroots dollar. As Southern rappers we were already at a handicap. Any hip-hop not coming out of New York or California was deemed unworthy. The hip-hop elites didn't think Southern rappers could be good lyricists and storytellers. Scarface was the only emcee thus far getting that kind of recognition. Goodie Mob, OutKast, and other Atlanta acts were putting in work and not getting the credit they deserved. The West Coast faced much the same hardships before they broke out the gate and were sitting on top of the hip-hop throne. Ironically, East Coast rappers were playing in our backyard, but not showing us any love.

Although rappers and producers were always flocking to do

shows in Miami, local rappers didn't get to share in the spot-light. A lot of big records came out of Miami. Out-of-towners stole our records and made them theirs. People weren't return-ing the love we showed them. Most people don't even know KC and the Sunshine Band came out of Miami. It's safe to say Miami was a forgotten stepchild on the hip-hop front. We were seen as nothing more than the folks who brought booty-shaking music. I wanted to shine a light on the other part of my city. I wanted to take folks to Overtown, Opa-locka, Ghouls, Liberty City, and the other ghettos. I wanted to introduce the world to that raw Miami shit. No other emcee was like me and no other city was like mines. That's right. There wasn't nann nigga in hip-hop like Trick Daddy.

37

"Nann"

In 1998, when I first showed everyone the lyr-
ics to "Nann," the consensus was that it would never get played
on the radio. People thought the lyrics were just too raunchy, with
more references to private parts and what to do with them than
in a sex-education class. Luke already had Congress all over him.
I had already told Ted upon signing me that no one was going
to make me change what I had grown used to. I was going to
show my gold grills and do what I do. I wasn't one of those flashy,
drenched-in-glitter, made-for-TV rappers. If the critics didn't like
it, they could kiss my black ass. People felt my music because it
was believable. I was just a two-time convicted felon that could
rap that wanted to show the world the circumstances that made
me who I was. After some heated rebuttals, everyone got on

board, but I wanted to add a twist to the song. I needed a partner in crime, so to speak. It's safe to say Miami girls got the most sass and attitude of any females around. You can't find a more ride-or-die chick than a Miami girl. They're the definition of what I call ghetto but classy. Hollywood's ex-girlfriend Katrina was all the above. After leaving high school, she was trying her hand at cosmetology school and stripping on the side. I approached her with the lyrics to the song, and she initially thought I was crazy.

"Trina, there isn't another bitch that can represent on this song like you," I told her.

She finally agreed. We started pushing the record in strip clubs. It's the best venue to break records because guys follow whatever music women like. Strippers certify hot music. Besides, I didn't have to harass some well-known radio personality for airplay. Strip club deejays are always open to new music. Then we hit the road. We piled inside a rented white, fourteen-passenger van and hit small Southern towns to promote the song.

Soon the hook to "Nann" was blaring out of car stereos. All the clubs were playing it. The record became the first Southern rap song to get major radio play in New York, the mecca of hip-hop. I landed my first national hit. The major labels came knocking down Ted's doors. Universal had signed that mega $30 million deal with Cash Money Records so all the majors were looking for that next big Southern act. With the stable of rappers we had, there was no question that Miami was the next town to take hip-hop to another level. Ted ultimately inked a deal with Atlantic Records. The money and everything that comes with it began piling in. The music video for "Nann" began popping up on MTV and BET, along with white spots on my face.

38

Hold On

At first I ignored the craterlike spots on my face. Black people tend to get dry skin, so I just went shopping for better lotion. As much as I rubbed the lotion, the spots just didn't go away. At times I couldn't go out in public. What I thought were spots were becoming large, painful, crusty sores that flared up sporadically. My friends tried not to stare when they spoke to me, but I could tell the spots had everyone sidetracked. It looked real bad.

Did you guys see the sores on Trick's face? He probably got the bug. You know, with all those groupies he slept with on the road. Yeah, he probably has the virus.

Back then, people weren't as educated about sexually transmitted diseases. So rumors about what caused the spots swirled.

The first thing people would say when someone appeared ill was that he had AIDS. I was worried. I hadn't lived the choirboy life. Magic Johnson had revealed his HIV status, and Eazy-E died of it in 1995. One of my brothers had also succumbed to the disease. AIDS was ravishing our community. If I did have HIV, I was determined to face it like a man. Hell, I had already survived riots, shoot-outs, and prison. I had seen everything but the wind.

Ted referred me to Dr. Betty Bellman. She ran a number of blood tests. Then she came back and told me I had discoid lupus.

"What!?" I asked, puzzled.

I had no idea what the hell lupus was or how to properly pronounce it. I was totally in the dark. When she broke it down for me, I thought my life had ended. This autoimmune disease caused my white blood cells to destroy themselves. My body was destroying itself. Ironically, I had spent so many years doing that in the streets now my anatomy followed suit. In its most severe form, the disease could reach my internal organs and kill me. My kidneys and liver were at risk. It caused my hair to fall out. The sun became my worst enemy. It's like an AK-47 with a double clip on it.

The doctor put me on medication, but I soon stopped because the side effects were unbearable. For a moment I decided that this was the end of the road. The news took me back to that place in the desert I mentioned earlier in this story, where hope leads you without a pot to piss in.

Fate would give me a taste of happiness, but somehow pain just always had to come knocking on my door. Then I started doing my research on the disease. I and so many other people were in the dark about lupus for a damn good reason. I found out that I wasn't alone with this condition. It killed hip-hop producer J Dilla.

The disease primarily affects black and Hispanic women. Little research has been done for the simple fact that it affects *us*. The powers that be don't want to invest money to come up with a cure for a disease that targets my community. A lady that I considered my grandmother has the disease so bad she's almost terminally ill. It's affected her bones and spinal cord. As many as 1 in 250 black women are likely to get the disease. I figured the same way I was using my experiences in the streets to spotlight conditions in the inner city, I could use my current condition to bring awareness to a disease that is unnecessarily claiming the lives of millions of my sisters. It can be an embarrassing disease to have, but I'm letting people know they don't have to suffer alone. I turned to family and friends for support. Joy became my anchor.

39

Sugar (Gimme Some)

ON THOSE LONG TRIPS PROMOTING MY FIRST AL-
bums, Trina's cousin Joy would tag along. If you let her tell
it, Joy, my wife to be, will say she was offended that I even
contemplated hitting on her. The woman was a mahogany
queen. I used to see her with Trina all the time, but I was too
busy in the streets to try my hand at holding down a relationship. Besides, Joy wouldn't have tolerated my large appetite
for the ladies.

But she was a chocolate sundae this brother had to go
add a banana to. Joy had the Miami attitude, but with a more
laid-back round-the-way-girl aura. She was the kind of girl you
could just kick back with at the beach. She wasn't trying to

be a diva. I knew if I was going to continue in the rap game, I needed an anchor. More important, I needed somebody that was levelheaded enough to cope with the pressures that come with dating a rapper. Joy never got insecure and jealous when we were promoting in strip clubs. She even befriended the strippers when they came over to hang all over us. Joy realized it was part of the game plan we came up with. She was a team player. Now don't get me wrong. My wife isn't a pushover. She's won't lose her cool often, but when she does, you better run for cover.

I could teach folks a thing or two about love. Love is about friendship. It isn't about who's wrong or right, to gain power or control over the other person. It's about two people getting together to make something sane happen in this crazy, messed-up place we call earth. The first thing anyone who wants to love someone must come to terms with is that no one's perfect. We all got flaws. Even your beloved pastor got some skeletons in his dusty closet. When you realize that, everything else in the relationship can be worked out. Once the other person's flaws aren't things that will make you throw him or her over a bridge, wedding bells will soon be around the corner. Our wedding ceremony was interrupted by me having to whup one dude's ass, but you get the point. It was hot, the food was running late, and folks got to acting up. Besides the beatdown, the wedding was a beautiful ceremony.

At first, I wasn't particularly Joy's type. She liked the college, suit-and-tie-wearing brothers. Joy didn't like ex-cons. Not in a million years did Joy see herself dating a guy with my track record. For that reason I liked her. She was innocent to my world. But like the old saying goes, opposites do attract, especially when one of those opposites was as persistent as I was. Every time I told Trina to set me up with Joy, she gave me the whole "Negro, please" look. I kept at it though. Finally, Joy got to know me for the person I was beyond the prison rap sheet. We've been best friends ever since.

40

God's Been Good

After the song "I'm a Thug" took me to the top of the rap plateau, I focused on my other true passion—kids. It's not a gimmick when I sing "Trick Loves the Kids." When you listen to the "Children's Song," that's some shit I'm rapping about from the heart. In my childhood, there wasn't much for me to smile about. Like me, so many kids are growing up with nightmares as opposed to playful memories. Adults need to stop making kids the scapegoats for all their mistakes. They don't deserve it.

I hate men who leave women in the dust to raise kids on their own. If you don't want the babies, I'll take every last one of them. Every time I see a teenage girl pushing a baby stroller toward a bus stop, I shed a tear. That's right. Trick Daddy's isn't immune to crying. I wish I could have an amusement park in my backyard. I'd invite all the kids from the projects across America.

My daughter, Imani, was born on October 31, 1995. I got her mother pregnant the same week I was released from prison. Then my son, Jayden, burst into the world on November 16, 2001. I'll take a bullet before I let them suffer the pain I went through at their age. I'm hoping to give them the support and guidance I never had. I want Imani to grow up to be a strong black woman and Jayden to be anything he wants. Look at Barack Obama. For the rest of my life, I'm going to regret not being able to vote for America's first black president. That's a privilege that was taken away from me as a convicted felon. But J won't have to sell drugs. I swallowed that pill for him. Now he can go ahead and possibly become the scientist that comes up with a cure for AIDS. Imani can be the next Oprah. That's one sister who I have the utmost respect for. I wish I could take her around my way to see how kids in the Beans and elsewhere in Miami are still suffering.

It's why I started my nonprofit organization. I spent so many years tearing down my community that I felt it was time to put something back into it. I know that's what Hollywood would have wanted. I'm not the richest rapper, but if I could give kids some school supplies to further their education, I believed I was able to move a mountain. It was high time Pearl left the Beans, so I got her a house in the suburbs. My niece Nene was the first person from Pearl's side of my family to go to college. I'm planning on sending my other niece Zuki after she graduates high school.

While I was preoccupied trying to uplift my community and

taking care of my family, the media chose to focus on my subsequent arrests. Bad habits are hard to break. The fame didn't change who I was. If someone tried to disrespect me, I was still going to run up side their head with a pistol. The money afforded more weed and cocaine.

Then in August 2004, more tragedy struck.

By the time I was at the height of my fame, Tater and Tronne were at the same plateau in the dope game. I can't help but wonder if things would have been different if I had been able to convince them to jump in on this rap game. However, we were cut from the same cloth. They were happy for me, but they were their own men. With the Feds crashing down on them, Tater cracked. I could never see one of us giving up the other. I guess the cops put the press on Tater, because he gave up everything. He told on the supplier, where the dead bodies were hid, and everything else. When the Feds caught up with Tronne, he didn't plan on going back to prison. They caught up to him on a bridge in Atlanta above the Chattahoochee River.

Tronne jumped. He missed the water and broke his neck on the rocks. The dope life had claimed another of my closest friends. I was devastated. I'm not sure if I could ever forgive Tater for turning on Tronne. Now more than ever I wanted to keep the circle around me close-knit. My older brother Chuck stepped in as my manager. He had managed to go to a Manhattan performing arts school he always dreamed about. Law school was next. But a baby in Miami brought him back home and full swing into the music game. In 2006, I decided to leave Slip-n-Slide and form my own label. I had made folks millions of dollars, but somehow my kids weren't playing with their kids. I guess it's easy to exploit a kid fresh out of prison with no options who is blessed with God-given lyrical skills. It was time for me to make my own money and be my own man. I went out and got a stable of artists I believed in. It means I've had to become a leader because they depend on me. I can't keep one foot on a banana peel and the other on solid ground.

I'd like Ice Berg, Fella, Murk Camp, Kasino, A-Dot, Chocolate City, Chronic, Beans, Bo, and Rick to go where I've been and further. Hopefully my younger brother Keyon gets out of prison in time to share in this dream. He was locked up for drug trafficking the same year I signed him to my fledgling label. That's the part of hip-hop folks don't focus on. Hip-hop saved my life. If it wasn't for these beats and rhymes, I would probably be staring you down with an AK-47 or be locked up or dead. All I did was give you my life in some verses. Now my crew can feed their kids with ghetto rhymes much the same. Hip-hop allows young black men to come together and create an avenue for those around us. I've seen brothers that graduated Harvard hit a glass ceiling in the corporate world. Imagine the chances for a brother with a rap sheet.

Sadly enough, the same lack of hope in Miami that sent me raising hell in those streets still exists. Liberty City street corners are still dotted with vacant lots and dilapidated stores. The Beans is still infested with the dope holes. But nowadays, the fiends can't even afford to buy the dope. People are still hurting in the hood. If the powers that be don't do something about it, crack is going to make the biggest comeback ever in Miami. Instead of blaming hip-hop for the problems in the black community, society could turn to it as a savior.

41

Tears of a Grown Man

I HAVE LESS MONEY AND WORSE CREDIT THAN THE average rap superstar. My court cases and those of my comrades bled me dry, but I'd like to see us rappers take care of the communities whose life we rap about. I'd like to hold a town hall meeting for the young brothers out on the block. I'd tell them they can be bigger and better than me. I was once where they were. I was on that corner with that work on me. I was once broke and fucked-up. Hell, at times I forgot to wash my ass out there on the corner. I wrote this book on behalf of myself and the brothers I came up with to let the young brothers know they don't have to suffer the pain we did. Opportunities are out there for a black man. A black boy can grow up to become president in this motherfucker. He won't have to stare down a life sentence.

Black has been locked up since 1989 and I've never heard him make an excuse or blame anyone for his situation. I've never heard him talk bad about his partner and codefendant, Shrimp, whom he's serving life with. When we speak, he's always amused at the new gadgets out on the market. If he ever gets out, I'll have to teach him how to use an iPhone. In many ways I owe him my life.

I ask one thing of the rappers who choose to mislead our kids while becoming pawns for an industry with no good intentions for our community.

Go shoot yourself. Slit your wrists. Hip-hop was our escape out this hell called the projects. It's not okay to write rhymes that make kids believe college isn't the place to be. We have the entire world dancing and jiving to the rhythm of our pain while AIDS and incarceration destroy our community.

Some would say Trick Daddy is a hypocrite for speaking some righteous shit. My response is, listen to the entirety of my albums. As an artist I can only paint the picture society presents. Brothers, take care of your kids. Stop leaving them for the streets to devour.

The coke life and the pain it causes is real. Those of us lucky enough to escape it live with lifelong nightmares. I'm sure the drugs I used to chase away those demons affected my lupus. Maybe the dope I sold caused someone to overdose. It may have left a child orphaned. It may have caused an addict to rob, even kill, his mother for money to get high. What if one of the bullets that left our AKs during shoot-outs killed a little girl or boy? She may have grown up to become the next Michelle Obama. That boy may have grown up to be Barack. I wish all the made-for-television, studio hard-core rappers would think about all that when they sit to write some make-believe cocaine rap.

Rappers, let's get together and build some community centers. Some child-care centers would be dope. I've always wanted to open a night-care center so the single mothers could go have fun while someone watches the kids. Mama gotta have a life too.

I'd like to tell my brothers who stay hustling in the street to deal with the consequences. Understand that when you put your hands on that white girl, there's a good chance her father will lock you in a six-by-nine-foot cage for the rest of your fucking life. Don't take down everyone with you to avoid that alternate ending. You made that choice. You made that bed. Now lay in the motherfucker.

In closing, I'd like to clarify something. I answer to God, because He's the only one I have to answer to when I leave this Earth. I'm trying to get into His big house, so I have work to do to earn my bunk. The media likes to criticize me for boasting that I'm a thug. They don't understand my definition. A thug isn't someone dressed in baggy jeans and Timberland boots ready to pistol-whip your ass. A thug is someone who stands on his own. He lives by the decisions he makes and accepts the consequences. Most problems stem from the fact that most people don't know who they are. A thug is comfortable in his own skin. I wear mine like a glove.

Printed in the United States
By Bookmasters